Tantra Mantra Yantra

The Tantra Psychology

Sri Garib Das Oriental Series No. 332

Tantra Mantra Yantra

The Tantra Psychology

S.K. Ramachandra Rao

Sri Satguru Publications

A Division of

Indian Books Centre
Delhi, India

Published by
Sri Satguru Publications,
Indological and Oriental Publishers
A Division of
Indian Books Centre
40/5, Shakti Nagar,
Delhi-110007
India

First Edition; Delhi , 1979
Second Edition : Delhi , 2008

ISBN 81-7030-899-2

Printed at Sachin Printers, Delhi

CONTENTS

Introduction **1**

The Tantrik Tradition **10**

The Psychic Structure **26**

Serpent Power and Mystic Fire **38**

Adepts and Attitudes **48**

The Ideological Basis **57**

Source Material **63**

Another Angle **71**

Mantra **85**

Specimens of Mantras **94**

References **97**

LIST OF PLATES

Santi-Yantra 7

Yantra-Raja 25

Ganapati-Yantra 27

Shadgunya-Yantra 28

The Higher Reaches of Kundalini 31

Muladhara-Chakra 33

Swadhishṭḥana-Chakra 33

Maṇipūra-Chakra 33

Anāhata-Chakra 36

Vishuddha-Chakra 37

Ājña-Chakra 37

Sahasrāra-Chakra 46

Swastika-Maṇḍala 47

Nāḍi-Maṇḍala 47

Agni-Stambhana-Yantra 54

Vasikara-Yantra 55

Kali-Yantra 66

Mukti-Mandara 70

Bala-Yantra 74

The Sacred Vase (Kalaśa) 83

The Hum Maṇḍala 83

The Maṇi-Chakra 84

Simple Yantra 92

INTRODUCTION

The study of the *Tantra* has suffered from two chief disadvantages. The enthusiasts have sought to project an image of it that is at once so highly esoteric and mystical that the scholar who has a modest opinion of his own intellectual abilities is easily scared away. The opponents, on the other hand, seek so to highlight the antinomian and obscene elements in the cults claiming to be Tantrik that the good citizen who has an eye for decency shies from it. Very few are aware that while the former attitude is unjustified, the latter is unwarranted. It is true that some Tantrik texts work with extremely abstract ideas and employ elaborate, and sometimes irrelevant, symbolism. It is also true that some Tantrik rituals as described and practised are wholly outlandish and obviously abominable. But these are deviations and perversions, altogether alien to the spirit and core of the *Tantra* ideology.

The Tantra was in origin folk, and the elements of abstraction were naturally minimal. It concerned itself with the normal man and pertained to his daily life. There was an unmistakable emphasis on the individual in this culture, contrary to the collective orientation of the Vedic tradition; but extravagance or eccentricity in individual behaviour was never suggested, encouraged or accepted. And Tantrik culture was bound rather with the ideal of 'quiet contemplation' than with the goal of 'joyful life', here or here after that we find reflected in the Vedic hymns. In fact, the Vedic temperament of buoyant and ecstatic involvement was to a great extent tempered as a result of Tantrik impact, as can be seen in the Upanishadic ideology. The Tantra is neither so forbiddingly esoteric nor so nauseatingly bizarre: it is a simple, wholesome approach to the problem of good living in a world of mixed forces.

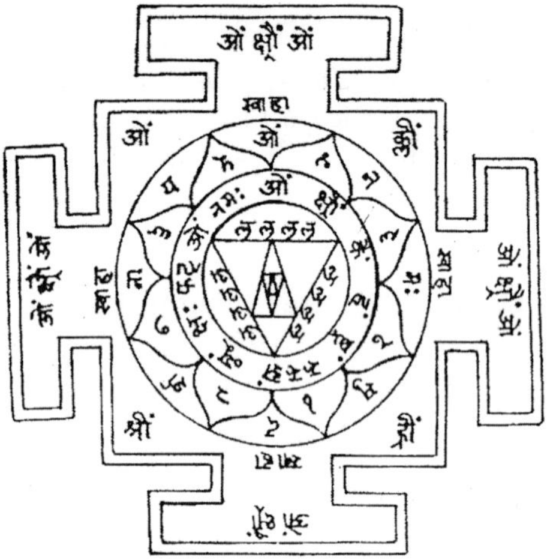

NARASIMHA-YANTRA, for dispelling danger (with the Mantra)

The expression 'tantra' has been variously derived and differently explained. It is taken to signify a system of thought, a body of practices, or a collection of books. Like the other word, Yoga, this word too means many things, both common and un-common, both normal and abnormal. As will be explained later, the original meaning appears to have been in the context of weaving on a loom: it was a vocation-derived word. Tantra is the loom whereon the threads are 'spread out' or 'extended' (root *tan*); it also meant the pattern or design that emerged out of this spreading or extension. Or it simply meant "explanation" (*'tattriti dhātoriha dhāraṇārthat'*). In the latter sense, it stood for a book or a chapter thereof, where arguments and explanations brought out a theme (like *Shashṭhitantra*), or stories illustrated a point (like *Pancatantra*). Originally referring to individual manuals, it came in course of time to stand for a whole literature of religio-magical treatises. More significantly, 'tantra' suggested the act of spreading out or the process of extension: techniques, methods, practices, tricks. The expression thus came to mean skill or competence in combining the methods and techniques.

We have an interesting definition by an eminent authority, Katyayana: "Tantra is the co-occurrence of actions". That is to say, it is an organisation of behavioural acts, a synthesis–exactly what Yoga means. Ayurveda makes use of the word 'tantra' in the sense of 'body', and another word '*yantra*' in the sense of its machinery. Body is a collection of organs (*angas*), an organization of forces (*dhatus, doshas* and *malas*), and a pattern of becoming. Even in its extended sense, '*yantra*' means a geometrical pattern, a synthesis of lines and 'seed-letters', a total representation. And 'mantra' likewise is an organization of sound-systems such as letters and words with some uncommon potency, namely a magic formula. Tantra technically is a process of relating the unusual patterns (*yantra*) with uncommon formulae (*mantra*). Basic to both these patterns and formulae is the belief that the human body is the ground where they operate. Yantras are merely extensions or externalisations of the forces imagined as working within the individual; and Mantras are in the nature of concretizations or formalisations of the vibrations occurring within. Tantra refers to the common field wherein these forces and vibrations operate, *viz.*, the body, not the gross physical body alone, but the 'dummy' body unseen though elaborate, and effective though invisible.

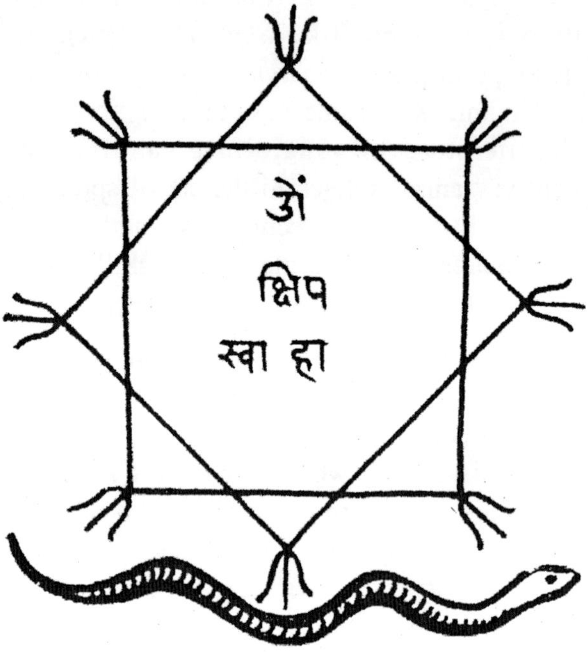

VISHAHARA-YANTRA, for snake-bite

That the body we can see and touch contains within it a dummy body we can neither see nor touch is a very ancient thought, common to most people in the world. The Tantra ideology developed this thought into an internal dynamics, a sort of psychical energetics within the individual. Thus the individual context became significant in the Tantrik tradition : instincts, impulses, aspiration and inhibitions of the individual were sought to be so organized that they functioned effectively, purposefully and unitarily. By such reorganization of the internal forces one not only overcomes the natural limitations but heightens the natural efficiency.

The actions involved in this organization or reintegration are the 'rituals', symbolic and suggestive. This pattern of actions corresponding to the pattern of the inner field-forces is what is meant by Tantra : and the yoking of actions to the field-force within is Yoga. The two expressions, Tantra and Yoga, emerged from the same source, and are meaningful in the same context.

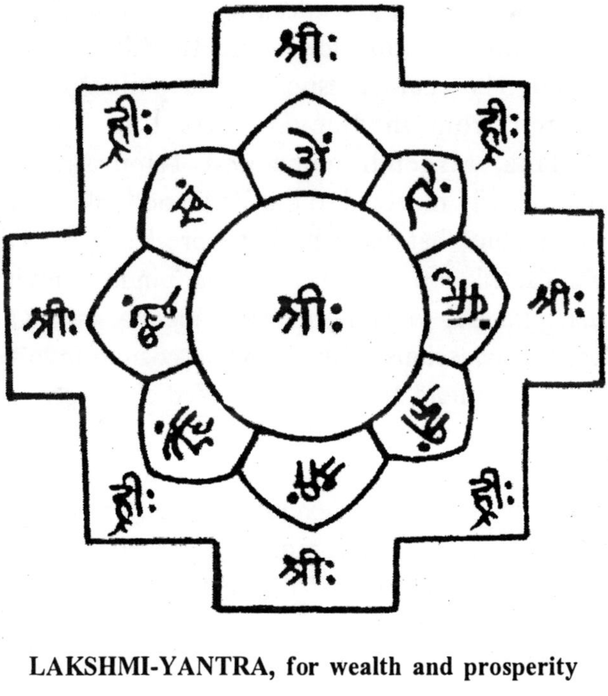

LAKSHMI-YANTRA, for wealth and prosperity

The Tantrik tradition thus focussed its attention on the individual; his physical structure, mental mechanism, modes of consciousness, and organismic motivations. The Vedic tradition, on the other hand, concerned itself mainly with the cosmos, subject to the capricious forces which are however amenable to coercion. The early Tantrik tradition did not stretch its imagination beyond the immediate surroundings of the individual. And at a later date when, under Vedic influence, it came to develop an interest in the world beyond, it comforted itself with the conviction that microcosm was essentially homologous with macrocosm. The cosmos was merely an extension, if not a projection, of the individual; the universe was in fact contained within the individual.

When we find similar ideas in the Upanishadic phase of Vedic literature, influence of the Tantrik ideology is to be inferred. The characteristic Tantrik philosophy, as can be gleaned from mediaeval texts like Tantraloka, Saradatilaka, Mrgendragama and Tripura-rahasya is doubtless heavily indebted to the Vedic outlook, although it contains a core that goes back to pre-Vedic times. The classical Tantrik concepts such as bija, bindu, samvit, kala, mandala, prakasa, vimarsa, ahamta, idamta, and Kancuka are clearly concessions to the growing cosmic involvement as a result of interaction with the Vedic thought system. Even when this involvement came to pass, the interest in the individual was not compromised. In the individual two aspects of life attracted the exclusive attention of the Tantra : breathing and sex. In common with primitive thought elsewhere, the Tantra feared that exhalation of the bodily air and ejaculation of the seminal fluid were tantamount to expenditure of life energy and hastening of death. In order to prolong life, it was considered necessary to restrain breath and arrest the seminal discharge. Pranayama techniques of breath control and procedures like yoni-mudra and vajroli-mudra to prevent 'the bindu reaching fire' (ejaculation) were advocated in some Tantrik texts. A text, the date of which is uncertain, Gorakshasamhita, brings out the intimate relationship between the breath (*prana*) and the semen (*bindu*); the two are in fact equated. It is understandable that the yoga-tantra complex attempted to understand sex and to harness the sexual drive to reach spiritual objectives.

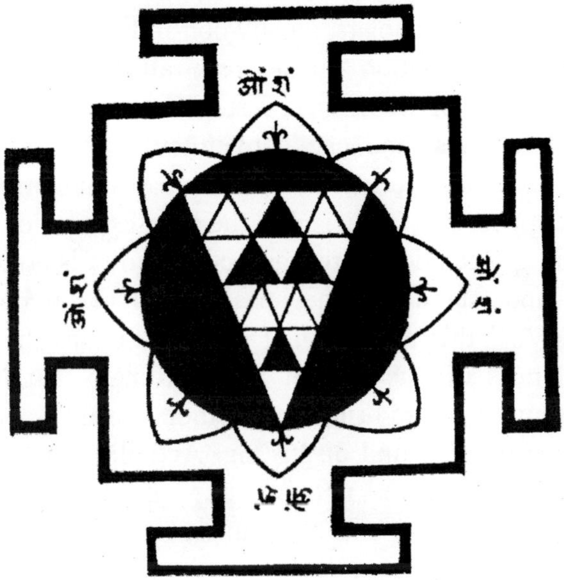

SANTI-YANTRA, used in rites for pacifying evil influences

Employment of sex imagery is no doubt frequent in the Tantrik lore. But it worked both ways–making it adorable and making it abominable. Sex in itself is neutral, like the air we breathe; and it is natural. Its expression depends upon individual maturity, motivation and mental habits. The several erotic and orgiastic cults that are at once enigmatic and seductive to the sophisticated Indologist grew out of certain unhealthy motivations and anti-social tendencies. But such cults do not suggest the essential orientation of the Tantra.

The attempt to discover, recognise and emphasize mystic meanings in what are patently absurd and outlandish has some times exceeded reasonable limits. The secret societies devoted to exotic and unbridled sexual indulgence (*guhyasamaja*) and to murderous crimes have masqueraded as esoteric Tantrik cults, and to an extent have got away with it. There are scholars, mostly non-Indian, who seriously explain that copulation "makes respiration rhythmical and aids concentration: it is, then, a substitute for pranayama", and they always, and can conveniently, cite in support Tantrik texts of uncertain date and dubious authority. They make it appear that eroticism is the very essence of Tantra; and their appreciation of this aspect of Tantra is not entirely one of understanding. The attractively got up books on 'Tantrik Art' that are flooding our book-shops these days are instances of this fact. It is unfortunate that in these circumstances Tantra brings to the Indian mind associations which are horrible and disgusting. Actually, however, sex in Tantra is employed not for direct gratification, but for 'reversal' (*paravrtti*) and restraint (*samyama* or *dharana*).

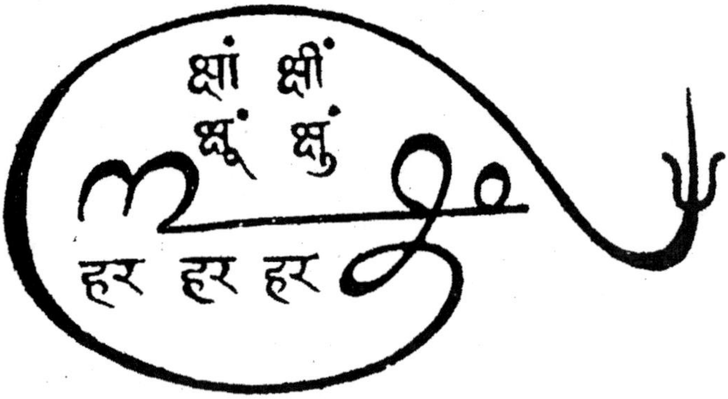

ROGA-HARA-YANTRA, for curing consumptive ailments

Tantra is not to be construed as a collection of mystic cults holding unusual ideas; it is a simple, serious, sober and realistic philosophy of life, which takes into consideration our normal impulses and aspirations. Samkhya-Yoga,

Ayurveda and the early Upanishadic texts more truly represent the Tantrik tradition than all the mystifying cults that commonly go by that name. In fact, regulated but effective living, eschewing excesses, was the basic Tantrik outlook. Preservation of health, acquisition of power to live effectively, and safeguarding of the community from individual aggression were the three objectives that were invariably emphasized. Control of breathing was meant to secure the first two objectives, and control of impulses, especially the sexual, took care of the third. There was considerable experimentation and theorizing before the methods were stylized and set as norms. The employment of medicinal and psychodelic drugs, alchemical techniques, and attempts at sex-sublimation were included in the experimentation.

THE TANTRIK TRADITION

The earliest employment of the expression 'tantra' occurs in the RgVeda[1] (although the occurrence is solitary). The context is the evulgar' trades that the lay-folk with unrefined speech take to, but not the learned or Soma-extracting priests. The word 'tantra' is used here along with 'work'. Sayana, in his commentary on the above, explains that 'tantra' is an agricultural implement (plough or loom) which is 'spread out' or 'elaborated' (*vistarayanti*), or merely 'worked' (*kurvanti*). Atharvaveda[2] used the word more specifically in the sense of 'loom'; and Panini takes the word 'tantraka' to mean a piece of cloth just taken out of the loom[3]. It is possible that this was the original connotation of the word. But it soon moved out of its shell, and came in course of time to signify a system composed of aspects, as for instance in Apastamba[4] (four or five centuries before Christ). This line of development is intriguing because it had already acquired a ritualistic involvement. Apastamba's commentator explains that it is a ritual procedure with multiple details. A curiously extended meaning in the same context is furnished by Sabara, an equally ancient authority: "when what is performed but once serves many purposes–even as a lamp lit up in the midst of priests".[5] However, the precise ritualistic import is more suggested than evident here. What perhaps was meant is that in the event of one being unable for some reason to go through the entire sequence of rituals, performance of a detail thereof would suffice to bring about the desired fruit. Alternately, it referred to some detail which is employed in diverse sequences in the self-same manner but with different benefits.

SVARNA-BHAIRAVA-YANTRA used in Alchemy

Tantra as a practical discipline appears to be a later interpretation. The Samkhya, for instance, styled itself as a 'tantra'; and Samkara (latter part of Sixth Century) recognises it as such;[6] Pancaratra was known as 'Sattvata-tantra'.[7] Kautilya (about 300 B.C.) uses the word in the sense of fundamental canons employed for explaining and expounding a system of thought.[8] This interpretation appears to have gained ground, and 'tantra' came specifically to mean a well-organized body of thought, with its own logic and rationale. It was even looked upon as tantamount to 'authority' or 'tradition'. But the word was still used rather sparingly with reference to the orthodox systems. Kullukabhatta's (around A.D. 1200) distinction between Vedic tradition and Tantrik tradition[9] was the prevailing view in the mediaeval ages. In many works, the term 'nigama' stands for the Veda and 'agama' for the Tantra. That the ritualistic import lingered on even when Tantra came to signify a 'discipline' is brought out by the references in some Puranas and in the Bhagavata that speak of three kinds of worship, Vedic, Tantrik and mixed.[10]

It can safely be assumed that at first the differences between the Vedic tradition and the Tantrik tradition were almost irreconcilable. Each camp looked upon the other as antagonistic, perverse and purposeless. If the Puranas proclaimed that the Tantras were prepared only in order to confound the wicked (*dushtanam mohanarthaya*), the Tantras like Kularnava claimed that a Tantra is like an honourable house-wife (*kulavadhu*) while the Veda with its accessories like Puranas and Sastras, is like a common harlot (*samanya-ganika*). The orthodox view, projected mainly by Kumarila (early sixth century), holds that Tantra was meant for the degenerate, the uneducated, the fallen, or the infirm, and that its rituals were fraught with dangers of all sorts. But the Tantrik enthusiasts held, and hold even now, that the Vedas, being antiquated, cannot lead to much good.[11] There was obviously a struggle for ascendance, and each tradition geared itself up to meet the needs of both the folk and the elite. And in the process, inevitably, each modelled itself after the other, assimilated the attractive particulars of the other, and attempted to secure the authority and support of the other. The Tantrik adherents sought to show that the tantra had Vedic foundation, Vedic sanction and Vedic authority. The Vedic puritans took over many of the hand-gestures (*mudras*), spells (*mantras*) and magic designs (*mandalas*) that the Tantriks employed, together with their methods of exposition. The new attitude is made clear by Apararka's counsel in his gloss on Yajnavalkya-Samhita that the Tantras should not be condemned outright, although they are not entirely valid or uniformly authoritative.

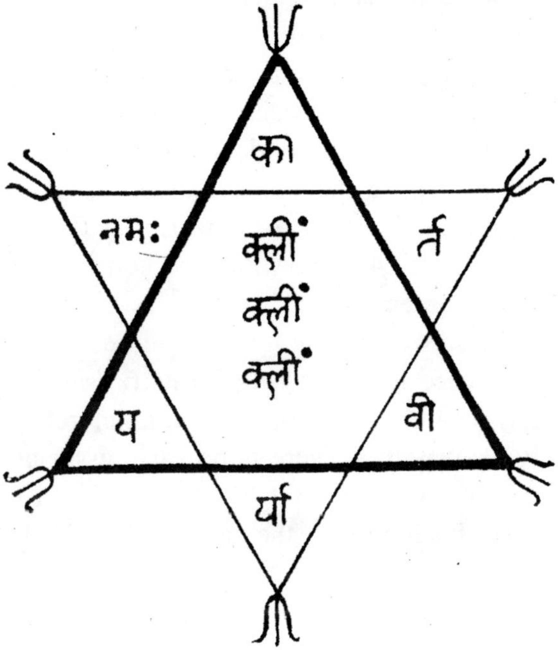

KARTAVIRYA-YANTRA for recovering lost property

The reconciliation between the two divergent traditions was partly effected by the orthodox authorities affiliating the Tantra to the 'Saubhagyakanda' of Atharvaveda, and the Tantrik writers relying heavily on Vedic texts like Taittiriya-aranyaka and describing their scriptures as continuation of the Upanishadic tradition.[13] The Vedic rituals adopted numerous Tantrik details and the Tantra abandoned its cruder cultic ideology in favour of the austere aspirations of the Upanishads.

The transformation of the Vedic hymnal Gayatri into a feminine divinity is an illustration to the point. In the

Veda, the celebrated solar hymn (known as *Gayatri*) occurs at several places (*e.g.* Rg-Veda 3,62,10; Yajur-Veda 3,35; 22,9; 30,2; 36,3) and is so called because "the hymn saves the one that recites it" (*gayan-tam-trayata iti*). The hymn is actually known as gayatra, and one who has mastered it is gayatrin (or *gayatri*). It is a masculine noun (comparable to dehi, "one who has a body", or dhani, "one who has wealth") and is used as such in the Vedic context (as, for instance, in RgVeda, 1.10.1, "*gayanti tva gayatrino*"). Gayatri is also a Vedic metre (with 24 units) which is frequently employed, although the nomenclature 'gayatri[4] is confined to the above-mentioned hymn. The hymn is addressed to the Sun (Savita, and hence it is also called Savitri "savitur iyam"). Manu (early centuries A.D.), for example, refers to this hymn only as 'Savitri'. There is no early association with any feminine deity at all. But the Atharva-Veda (19.71.1) had described this hymn as "the mother of the Veda" (*veda-mata*), in the sense of being the source and support. This heralded the course by which the simple solar prayer developed into a stylized, iconic goddess with a definite Tantrik framework. And there came into being specific gayatris for several gods and goddesses, which the Vedic worshippers as well as the Tantrik adherents freely used. There were also characteristically Tantrik gayatri (like "Om Adyayai vidmahe, Tripurayai dhimahi, tan no Kali pracodayat" and "Om *Mahadevyai ca vidmahe, Vishnupatnai, ca dhimahi, tan no Lakshmih pracodayat*") which were incorporated in standard Vedic worship. The Vedic gayatri was even employed in witchcraft and sorcery under general Tantrik directions (cf *Vishnudharmottara*, 1.165.55-63, for abhicara purposes, *"viparitam prayojayet"*).

Although the two thus met, each in its essentials continued to be uncompromising. This is how, in isolated areas, the original and rigid Tantrik and Vedic prejudices persist even to this day.

The credit for bringing together Vedic wisdom and Tantrik tradition should go to the great Samkara (late sixth century). His name is honoured not only in the Vedantic tradition but in the Tantrik tradition as well. Besides the well-known commentaries on the triple source of Vedantic wisdom (*Upanishads, Brahma-Sutras,* and the *Gita*), he is said to have written the celebrated Tantrik works, Prapancasara and Saundarya-lahari, and also others like Cintamani-stava (according to Bhaskararaya, and listed in Burnell's Catalogue of Tanjore MSS), Lalita-trisati-bhasya (which is supposed to have been prepared in Kashmir) and Tara-pajjhatika (dealing with the worship of Tara, the great Tantrik Savioress). As in the traditional Vedantic line of teachers, in the Tantrik line also, he was preceded by sages (like *Vasishtha, Sakti, Suka* and *Vyasa*) and by historical personages, (like *Gaudapada* and *Govinda*). However, in the Tantrik tradition Govinda does not immediately follow Gaudapada: there are four or five other teachers that intervene. Gaudapada and Govinda are described here as great Tantrik adepts. Besides the well-known Karika on the Mandukya Upanishad, Gaudapada is said to be the author of two Tantrik works, Sakti-Sutras (according to *Bhaskararaya*) and Subhagodaya-stuti (on which the great *Tantrik* writer *Lakshmidhara* has commented). He is reputed to have been partial to Sri-Vidya school of Tantra. Govinda, about whom we know very little in the Vedantic tradition and whose Vedantic works have not survived at all (if indeed he wrote any), was a great name in the Tantrik tradition. A very well-known work Jayadratha-yamala is ascribed to his authorship. Recovered from Nepal, this work suggests the impact of Trans-Himalayan cults on the purely Indian Tantrik tradition. Tara was probably introduced into the mainland of India from the Himalayan regions. And the ascription of a manual of Tara-worship to Govinda's successor, the great Samkara, is not altogether fantastic. We know that the great temple at Kanchi (in South India) with which Samkara's association was both continuous and intimate, was dedicated originally to Tara. There were several Tara shrines in the country at one time, and Samkara's name is connected with most of them. Samkara inherited from Gaudapada his interest in Sri-Vidya, and popularized the worship of the Mother-Goddess in the form of the mystic diagram Sri-Cakra. Unlike in the Vedantic tradition, Govinda becomes in the Tantrik tradition an effective teacher of Samkara's.

Samkara's immediate disciple, Padmapada, figures in both the traditions. In the Tantrik tradition, he is credited with a commentary on his master's Prapanca-sara, entitled Sambandha-dipika. There were other disciples of Samkara like Bodha, Girvana, Ananda, Visnu-sarma, Laksmana-desika (the author of *Sarada-tilaka,* a standard Tantrik work), Mallikarjuna of the Vindhyas, Trivikrama of Jagannath-Puri, Sridhara of Bengal and Kapardin of Banaras, who helped spread the Tantrik teachings in different parts of the country. The establishment of the four or five amnayas (cultic centers) in the different corners of India, which is ascribed to Samkara, is not without an interest. These are all associated with Sakti-pithas (Tantrik Centers) and rituals conducted here have an unmistakable Tantrik background. In fact, the very concept of amnaya is a Tantrik one; Sri-Vidyarnava-tantra for instance, speaks of five amnayas, urddhva (upland), purva (eastern) pascima (western) uttara (northern) and dakshina (southern).

Samkara's interest in Tantra was not accidental. The practical significance of the doctrine of Advaita-vedanta that he espoused and expounded can never be understood or appreciated unless we take into account Samkara's Tantrik leanings. Advaita was not meant to be a mere intellectual discipline; it was not only an approach to Reality (a *darsana*) but a means to reach it (an *upasana*). When the Upanishads distinguished two kinds of knowledge, the higher (*para*) and the lower (*apara*) they included all Vedic lore in the latter.[14] The position was identical with the Tantrik outlook; and the distinction between transcendental and transactional levels of Reality which the Mahayana Buddhists (principally the *Madhyamikas* after Nagarjuna) as well as Gauda-pada and Samkara accepted can be traced to a Tantrik source. Both the 'levels' are in fact field-forces or powers, the latter binding, and the former freeing, the individual. They are the equivalents of the unconditioned Brahman and the conditioned in Vedanta, of the moksa and dharma in Mimamsa. It was Samkara's view that Advaita-upasana pertains to the former while the Sri-Cakra-puja to the latter. The involvement of Sri-Cakra in all the pontificates and shrines with which Samkara was connected (like the Sarada shrine of Sringeri, the Kamakshi shrine of Kanchi and the Mukambika shrine of Kollur) was the natural outcome of the recognition that Tantra is the translation of theory into practice.

It would appear that Gaudapada prepared the way for Samkara. It is significant that Samkara singles out, from among several predecessors that he cites, Gaudapada for a unique description: 'knower of tradition' (sampradaya-vit).[15] And his regard for tradition is expressed by the following remark of his: "Although acquainted with all scriptures, if one is ignorant of tradition he should be disregarded as a fool." [16] What then is the tradition, that, according to him, Gaudapada knew? Not the Vedic tradition, for he severely criticizes the Mimamsakas who solely rely on Vedic wisdom or the Vedantic tradition that strictly follows the Vedic texts, for he criticizes also his predecessors (some of whom were *Advaitins*) like Brahmadatta, Bhartrprapanca and Bhartrhari, who answered this description. Gaudapada, however, was remarkable in many ways. He distinguished between transactional and transcendental levels of Reality, classified wisdom into absolute and relative, suggested the illusory nature of the phenomenal world (*maya*), and postulated the theory of transformation (*vivarta*). His position doubtless smacked of Mahayana Buddhism, and there are well-founded indications in the Karika that he favoured the Madhyamika view. But he insisted on the relevance of scriptural authority; and undertook to interpret an Upanishadic text. What he sought to show was that the views that had emerged from the Tantrik quarters (*viz.* the *Mahayana Buddhism*) were also the views of the Vedic sages. Gaudapada recognized the continuation of 'tradition' from Upanishads to Buddhism, and also recognised that the Upanishads had already incorporated the Tantrik ideas. This perhaps was the tradition that Samkara was referring to.

Gaudapada and Samkara thus reestablished the synthesis of the old Vedic tradition and the Tantrik tradition. It has been held that the Tantrik ideology is clearly reflected in the Taittiriya-aranyaka, a text that the Tantrik writers of Vedic persuasion frequently rely upon.[17] The very first section thereof is devoted to a ritual connected with the sage Aruna-Ketaka. There is an Upanishad, which probably grew out of this section, Arunopanisad, which projects the greatness of the goddess Aruna (also mentioned in *Vamakesvara-tantra*). Arunas were in fact a group of sages (like Ketus and Vatarasanas) whose origin was mythically traced to the carcass of Prajapati. The other groups (like the *Vratyas,*

Vaikhanasas, Valakhilyas and *Sramanas*) were likewise participants of both traditions, and their origin was traced to the different limbs of the same Prajapati. It is interesting in this connection to note that Samkara describes Gaudapada as a follower of Prajapati,[18] who perhaps symbolized the synthesis that Gaudapada and Samkara sought to re-establish.

The new synthesis was not without its justification. Both traditions had encouraged mystical tendencies in different periods, and were gradually moving away from popular hold. The movement that Gaudapada and Samkara spearheaded was in fact a reaction against the excessive mysticism of the Mimamsakas on the one hand and of the Mahayana Buddhists on the other, around the early centuries of the Christian era. The new movement appealed to reason and supported quietism. Iconic worship (*pratikopasana*) had already come to stay: the adherents of both traditions had favoured it, and therefore rituals of diverse types had sprung up. Quiet contemplation which was alike the essential feature of the two traditions was receding to the background. The Brahmasutra (4.1,3-12), however, suggested *'aham-graho-pasana'* (introverted absorption) as an alternative technique to iconic worship; and this had scriptural sanction as well as support from Tantrik ideology. Samkara's Advaita as an upasana was a natural development of this suggestion.

The Tantra is a collective expression : it comprises numerous tribal and regional cults, admitting of several systems of classifications. But it is interesting that all of them have certain common working principles such as the indispensability of a guru, the necessity of initiation (*diksha*), secretiveness of ritual performances, and employment of symbolism. In a sense, Tantra is most adequately described as 'symbolic wisdom, directly communicated through a teacher' (*sanketavidya guruvaktragamya*). Its symbolism presents a real difficulty for students of this lore, especially of Western extraction. We do not know precisely when this discipline allowed itself to be written down. But we have a mass of Tantrik manuals, digests, handbooks, instruction-sheets and picture-books right from the fourth or fifth century onwards till comparatively recent times, most of them in Sanskrit (sometimes in corrupt Sanskrit). The 'Tantra written down' is obviously paradoxical, for it is by definition what is got orally from the teacher, and there is a severe injunction that books are never to be substitutes for teachers. It is surprising that not only theoretical explanations, even instructions for actual practice (like *Sadhanamala, Sadhana-samuccaya* and *Sadhana-vidhi*) exist in hundreds. Probably, scholars could not resist the temptation to write; and when they were motivated by compassion for fellow-creatures (as the *Mahayana* and *Vajrayana Tantriks* ostensibly were) they had an additional incentive. But they were aware of the Tantrik prejudice against publicity, for the Tantra is essentially a confidential affair, strictly private to the practitioner and his master. In order to reconcile their urge to write with the injunctions against writing, they found an expedient method in employing 'symbolic speech'. They wrote no doubt in a language which all could read but few understand. This language, or rather the style of writing, is technically known as 'sandhabhasha' (or Sandhya-bhasha which is, however, erroneous): 'intentional language' (*Vidhusekhara Bhattacharya*), enigmatic language' (*Burnouf*), 'mystery-language' (*Kern*), 'language intentionel' (*Eliade*), or 'hidden sayings' (Max-Mueller).[19] It is obvious that the Tantrik tracts were originally meant only for private use, and for carefully limited circulation; the ritualistic presentation of a copy would invariably be accompanied by oral clarifications and essential explanations. For others, naturally, the writing made little sense; and when taken literally, it would either confound them, or lead them astray.

MANTRODDHARA-YANTRA for extracting the necessary Mantra

The strangeness of the language used in Tantra was also due to the fact that characteristic expressions were taken over when foreign cults were incorporated. The sixth century work Jayadrathayamala, recovered from Nepal, contains some mono-syllabic words (*ekakshara-samullapa*) described as those used by yoginis, and they are identified as the Trans-Himalayan dialects, 'Paisacha' and 'Bhota' (presumably Tibetan). The yoginis appear to have been mainly of non-Indian extraction. The Tantras of extra-Indian origin like the Maha-Cina-Tantra and the Nila-Sarasvati-Tantra mention that the yoginis employed the secret language (*sandha-bhasa*).

It is not only the language of the Tantrik texts that is symbolic. Tantra is in fact committed to a symbolism in a more essential particular. The source of this commitment is not far to seek. One of the basic propositions of Tantra is the primacy of the individual as the product and source of energy. The individual, in this view, is a miniature universe; macrocosm is not only contained within the microcosm, but has a certain essential parallelism with it. The forces that operate in the world are all dormant within the person

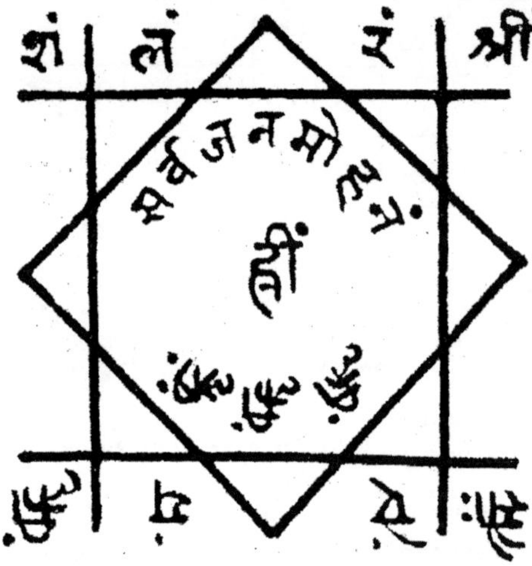

SARVAJANA MOHANA-YANTRA for skill in magic

functioning, however at a different plane. But when they are organized adequately and harmonized effectively, man would become the receptacle of some extra-ordinary power. The more practical and mundane forms of Tantra speak of mastery over elements and magical attainments (*siddhis*), but the more spiritual forms insist on 'great liberation even while alive' (*jivanmukti*) as the proper goal. The 'immortality' of the body, which was the Taoist and alchemical preoccupation all over the world, was also an objective in many Tantrik cults in India. Besides magic, sorcery and witchcraft, Indian enthusiasts also evolved exercises for tranquility and liberation. What is relevant for our discussion here is the series of techniques they developed which were meant to harmonize and channelize the psychic energy; and this goes by the name of 'sadhana'a sort of 'internal spiritual alchemy'.

The purpose of Sadhana is to transform the individual and to harness the energy that is locked up in the body and that normally conditions him to rather narrow and unsatisfactory conditions of existence, so that he begins to function more effectively, more meaningfully and more zealously. Naturally, therefore, Sadhana involves a set of exercises, physical (like breath-control and effective bodily postures) and mental (like contemplation, concentration and visualization). Sometimes extreme forms of asceticism or curious sexual practices are also included, rarely though. Rejection of convention, withdrawal from normalcy, performance of some gruesome and disgusting rites, and apparently perverse sexual indulgence are no doubt glaring features in many a Tantric cult; but it must be remembered that they are neither regarded as natural nor as strictly necessary for Tantric achievement. Even bodily postures are confined to a few elementary types, although hand-gestures and finger-manipulations (*mudras*) loom large. The main emphasis, however, is on mental exercises. Breath control is made secondary to, and the means of, thought control. And thought control is the gateway to gain mastery over psychic energy. Sadhana, whatever the variety of affiliation, is the procedure by means of which the four basic aspects of the individual, namely the vital current, mind, consciousness and energy, are mobilized and harmonized.[20]

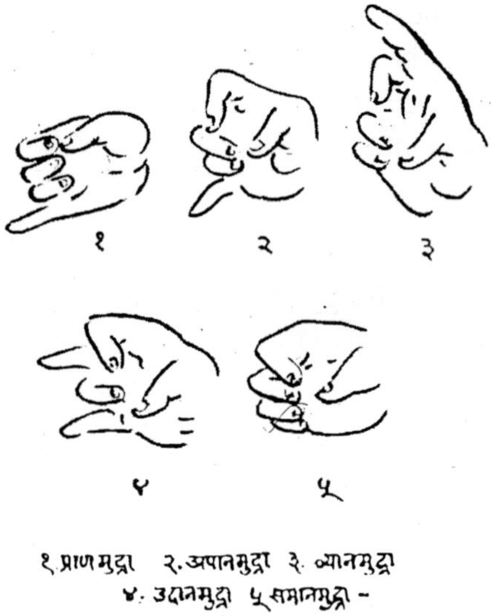

THE MUDRAS symbolising five vital functions (Pancaprana)

All practices are directed towards collecting and organising psychic energy. An early and common device that the Tantra employs is the 'mandala', the detail of Indian Psychology that stimulated Carl Jung's interest enormously. Mandala has been variously translated by experts as 'cosmogram', 'cosmogenic model', 'map of the soul', 'cosmic plan', 'symbol of Kosmos', and 'layout of the psyche.' Basically it is a visible geometrical design, frequently a circle (*cakra*), denoting the entirety of existence; the forces are symbolically projected on it and arranged according to an operational theme. It is a topological concept, involving the reconstruction of subjective space. Represented externally, it symbolises the layout of the entire earth; the central point signifying the mountain Meru, round which all the continents, subcontinents, realms and states of existence are arranged stylistically. But the world has meaning only as related to man and man is the chief concern of the Tantra. Each individual therefore absorbs the world into himself, or conversely gets himself absorbed into the world. The relating process that goes on in everyone of us normally does not 'center' the world properly in the individual, nor does it 'center' the individual in the world correctly. The Tantra recognises that all our misery is due to this improper centering, and sets out to teach the effective procedure for correct centering.

YANTRA-RAJA used in several rituals

THE PSYCHIC STRUCTURE

If the cosmos is extended in one dimension of space (*mahakasa*, physical space), the individual psyche is extended in another dimension (*cittakasa*, subjective space). The growing distinction between the two dimensions is the source of subject-object duality, which is fundamental to normal experience. The course of life is busily concerned with the almost impossible task of balancing the two dimensions or lines of stress, unaware of the fact that the two can really be unified only in the third dimension of space (*cidakasa*, the space of pure consciousness). The Mandala device seeks to center the dimensions neatly; it is therefore correctly described as 'a centering technique'. The human body is itself a mandala, the psyche being the dimensionless point at the very centre (*bindu*). Even as a point describes a circle in its spread, the psyche unfolds itself into a mandala. This inner space is projected on to the symbolic outer space (the material mandala as a design, a diagram, or a model), by a creative process of visualization. The hand-gestures and finger-manipulations (*mudra*) representing the bodily processes (*kaya*), the utterance of mystic formulae (*mantra*) representing verbal behaviour (*vak*), and symbolic diagrams (*yantra*) representing mental functions (*citta*) are aids in this process of projection. The Tantra makes extensive use of the imagery of seed (*bija*), sprout, evocation and tree. The external mandala is the soil, mantra the water, mudra the sun-shine and *yantra* the manure. The guarding of the external mandala by protective spells and devices is also attended to. In the words of Tucci: "A mandala delineates a consecrated place and protects it from invasion by disintegrating forces... it is much more than just a consecrated area that must be kept pure for ritual and liturgical ends. It is above all, a map of the cosmos. It is the whole universe in its essential plan, in its process of emanation and of reabsorption."[21] The Tantra design is always enclosed in a protective circle or square serving both as a contour and as a cover of defence. It is important that the practitioner should get into it and thereby become invincible, adamantine, and firm (*vajra*). For achieving this entrance

GANAPATI-YANTRA, a mandala used in the worship of Ganapati

into the mandala, one has necessarily to leave the normal world of distractions and fragmentations behind, and pass into an altogether different world of symbols and visualizations. Mandala's description as 'the mansion of gods and goddesses' is symbolic of higher life, conceptual and projected. The practitioner creates this symbolic world as an emanation from his own depths and as an expansion of his own consciousness; after the ritual or contemplation is over, he withdraws this symbolic sphere into himself. The latter process is technically styled 'reabsorption'; it is resumption of the normal and everyday coordinates of being, knowing and doing.

We mentioned that the body itself is a mandala, and that this was a basic premise of the tantra. There is a notion, held almost universally in India, that an individual has three bodies : a 'physical' body (*sthulasarira*), the 'mental' body (*subtle, sukshma-sarira*) and the 'causal' body (*karana-sarira*).[22] The physical body is made of the five elemental

SHADGUNYA-YANTRA, employed in the worship of Vishnu

forces, and is sustained by food. The mental body, on the other hand, is constituted by the vital currents, the organs of sensations and actions, mind and consciousness. This is no doubt founded on physical structures but its essential nature is psychological. The third body *viz.,* the causal, is not relevant to our discussion here. The physical and mental bodies, although distinct both by constitution and in function, are related to each other intimately and the points of contact are described as 'psychic centers' (*cakras*) and pictured as lotuses (*padmas*). Lotus is a flower that has caught the Indian imagination not only by its beauty and delicacy but by its large multiplicity of petals, vitality and purity. The element of sumptuous fecundity is not excluded from the concept.

Attempts, often fantastic, have been made to identify these centers with anatomical regions and physiological functions known to thc modcrn mind. But it is important to note that these do not belong to the physical body as such, nor to the mental structure as such. It is true that they are located (in the Tantric texts) along the brahmadanda or merudanda, by which we usually understand the spinal column. But the description of the column as encasing a subtle channel (known as *sushumna*) extending from the spinal base to the cranium is obviously abstract. Further, each center (also termed plexus or vortex) is looked upon as a network of very subtle, altogether invisible arteries (*nadis*). The human body is said to consist of seven hundred million of these arteries, some gross and others subtle, along which the vital currents flow continually in order to keep the body alive and active. The principal of these arteries is the sushumna (also called *avadhutika*), just mentioned, inside the merudanda (roughly corresponding to the spinal column) is a fine but hollow canal, extending from the region of the penis to the head, called 'diamond' (*vajra or vajrini*). Inside this is another artery, exceedingly fine like the thread of a spider's web, or as thin as the thousandth part of the hair; this is called 'the marvellous' (*citrini*). And this latter in its turn encloses the artery known as brahmanadi, the essential but highly abstract life-current.

The cakras are composed of networks of arteries, arranged along the sushumna. The Tantrik texts of the Hatha-yoga persuasion enumerate as many as thirty of such centers, ranging from the big toe of the foot to the top of the head.[23] Each of these has a characteristic colour, a number of petals (when pictured as a lotus), an elemental association, a particular sense-organ, an organ of action, a variety of the vital current (*prana*), a seed-syllable, a symbol, a male deity and his consort, and a representative animal.

Of these centers seven are regarded as especially important, six inside the body and one outside it. The last one, named sahasrara (after the picture of an inverted, thousand-petalled lotus, and known to Buddhists as ushnisa-kamala, the crown-lotus), is imagined to be located four finger-breadths above the crown of the head. Although outside the physical body, it is a part of the existential structure, but at its topmost level. Here is supposed to be the source of the 'liquid of immortality', the liquid that drips on the cranium continuously, thus making one alive and active. It is clearly a mystical center. The other six form a group, 'the six-centers' (*satcakra*), arranged in an order along the sushumna. The lowest in location is styled 'the root-basis' (*muladhara*), pictured as a triangular space, red in colour, within a square of yellow, right in the middle of the body: it is called 'the earth mandala'. Its physical location is said to be in the sacral plexus or perineum(?), or between the base of the genital organ and anus. It is the lower limit of the sushumna canal. Here, two other arteries, celebrated in Tantrik exercises, meet.

The higher reaches of Kundalini (The Thousand-petalled Lotus)

In Tantrik lore, the central sushumna is flanked on its left with ida and on its right with pingala, two subtle psychic arteries both arising from the "root-basic' center and running parallel and close to the sushumna until they cross, and the right-left position is reversed. The two arteries signify opposite poles; and they are described as male-female components within each individual. Ida (also called *lalana*) is the famous Indian river Ganga, pingala the equally famous river Yamuna; and sushumna is the hidden stream Sarasvati. The three together constitute the sacred triple-stream (*triveni*) commingling at the 'root-basic' center. Rudrayamala (6.49) speaks of ida as the moon, pingala as the sun, and sushumna as the fire. The imagery of sun and moon has been a persistent one in Tantrik literature; the Natha-Siddha Tantriks even wear large ear-rings symbolising sun and moon. Moon stands for Siva, the static but enduring element both in the universe and in man; it is the repository of nectar (*amrta*); its normal location is said to be the highest center (*sahasrara*); its white colour signifies the male aspect (*pandura-bindu-cakra*). Sun, on the other hand, is the dynamic but ever-changing element both in the universe and in man; it stands for Sakti, the female aspect, and is represented as 'reddish ovum' (*lohitabindu-maharajas*); it is located in the 'root-basic' center (*muladhara*). "In the muladhara is Sakti and in sahasrara Siva" (*muladhare vasate saktih sahasrare sadasivah*). Further, the ida and pingala arteries are described as possessing the following contrary characteristics: day, night; exhalation-inhalation; food (*upabhogya*)-consumer (*bhoktr*); vowel (*ali*)-consonant (*kali*); semen-ova; creation-destruction, prana-apana; samsara-nirvana. The opposing characteristics are all summarised in the moon-sun imagery: the moon has a cooling effect on the system while the sun dries up the system; one builds up the body and the other breaks it down. In mystical parlance, one determines the individual involvement in the phenomenal vortex, while the other burns up this bond and releases the individual.

But it would be an error to look upon man as a helpless victim of two contending forces. As a matter of fact, the two are complementary and make for a 'biunity' (Dr. Ananda K. Coomaraswamy's expression), a male-female configuration which is essential both for creation and release. In the ordinary individual, in the state of normalcy, unity is not recognised or consciously achieved; and hence the pain of

MULADHARA-CHAKRA

SVADHISHTHANA-CHAKRA

MANIPURA-CHAKRA

life. The union of ida and pingala at the lowest centre (where most of us mostly function) is described as the darkest phase of the moon (amavasya). Commingling with the hidden Sarasvati (*viz.*, the *susumna*), the triple-streams are here 'freed' (*muktatriveni*), that is to say, they flow separately. But when the individual takes up the Tantrik career, or practises Yoga, the openings of ida and pingala at the 'root-basic' center are blocked, and the currents are forced to move along the central sushumna. The three streams are now commingled into a unitary flow (*yukta-triveni*), which reaches its culmination in the center between the eye-brows. This is described as the brightest phase of the moon (*purnima*). In some texts, however, the expressions mukta and yukta with reference to the triple-flow (*triveni*) are used in a sense exactly opposite to the one mentioned above. The 'root-basic' center is described as 'joined' or 'yoked' (*yukta*) as regards the three streams, while the center between the eye-brows is described as 'freed' (*mukta*). The presupposition here is that the confluence of the three streams is responsible for individuality, while the cessation of that confluence, achieved by sadhana would release the individual from conditioned phenomenal existence.

The center located above the 'root-basis' is known as 'self-supporting' (*svadhisthana*), and is pictured as a colourless crescent, representing the water element, identified with 'prostatic plexus' (?), or located in the navel region. If the 'root-basic' center is the source of all desires, the 'self-supporting' centre provides all the excitement; the two together are responsible for the instincts of sex and survival. The psychological traits originating at this level (the vrttis) are given as: affection, suspicion, contempt, infatuation and cruelty. The third center, 'jewel-filled' (*manipura*), is said to be located in the lumbar or 'epigastric plexus'(?); it is more usual, however, to take it as a 'navel center' (*nabhipadma*). Red in colour, it signifies fire. The psychological traits associated with this center bring out the 'burning' character: shame, jealousy, fear, remorse and disgust.

Curiously, this center is spoken of as responsible also for sleep and thirst. The 'unstruck' (*anahata*) centre, situated in the heart and known as 'cardiac plexus'(?), is imagined as a hexagon with two interlacing triangles, greyblue in colour. The Buddhist texts, however, locate this center at the throat, and give its form as semi-circular and its colour as green. Associated with the element air, it provides the individual a subjective frame of reference, *viz*., an ego. Among the psychological traits originating here are hope, worry, effort, the feelings of 'I' and 'mine', arrogance, egoity, covetousness, double-dealing, indecision, regret, and discrimination. The perfectly 'pure' (*visuddha*) center, golden in colour and circular in shape (white disc in Buddhist texts), is located in modern accounts at the 'laryngeal plexus' (?), or at the junction of the spinal column and medulla oblongata behind the throat (located at the crown of the head by Buddhist authors). Governing the organs of expression and articulation, this center is associated with the following mental traits: faith, joyousness, guiltfeeling, restraint, respectability, friendliness, sorrow, agitation, enthusiasm and detachment.

The sixth center is styled 'allround understanding' (*ajna*); the Buddhist texts describe it as the 'third eye of wisdom', the center of formless contemplation. Situated between the eye-brows (or a little above), formed by two white petals representing sun and moon, this center governs efforts at concentration as well as states of trance. Some Tantrik texts call this center the highest house' (*paramakula*) and 'the breaking up of the triple-confluence' (*mukta-triveni*).

Although these six centers are the ones widely known and frequently enumerated in the Tantrik manuals, sometimes another center is mentioned, 'the center of mind' (*manascakra*). Located just above 'the center of understanding', this is said to be the secret center responsible for all perceptual processes and dream states. Above this center is 'the moon center' (*soma-cakra*), also infrequently mentioned. Said to be situated in the middle of the cerebrum, the psychological traits associated with this center are all morally positive and constructive: softness, courage, perseverance, humour, humility, concentration, poise, industriousness, emotional stability and generosity. This is the highest center within the psychophysical system, immediately below the one that is outside the system, *viz.*, sahasrara (described as 'the house without a support' *niralambapuri*).[24]

ANAHATA-CHAKRA

VISHUDDHA-CHAKRA

AJNA-CHAKRA

SERPENT POWER AND MYSTIC FIRE

It should be remembered that the concept of cakras is essentially esoteric. And, therefore, attempts at discovering the physiological correlates are bound to be both farfetched and misleading. The cakras are more properly different fields of psychological reality, and their 'petals' symbolise the dimensions thereof. Read, for instance, the following description of the four higher cakras, and their mystical significance becomes at once apparent: "The manipura is a lotus of 64 petals turned upwards, their colours being yellow, and the seed-syllable being Ah; the anahata is a lotus of eight petals, blue black in colour, turned downwards, the seed-syllable being *Hum; visuddha* has 16 petals of red colour turned upwards, with the seed-syllable Om; and the *sahasrara* has 32 petals all white in colour and turned downwards, the seed-syllable being *Ham*." This Tantrik account is slightly different from the Yoga account (which, for instance, gives the number of petals of the six cakras as 4, 6, 10, 12, 16 and 2 respectively, accommodating the fifty letters of the Sanskrit alphabet, and gives their seed-syllables as lam, vam, ram, yam, ham and om). The description is directly derived from visualizations, and not from imaginative reflection. The cakra ideology is thus a product of mystical contemplation, which taps the fundamental energy dynamics at work within our basic constitution.[25]

More significantly, the cakra ideology would be meaningless without reference to the more fundamental, if also more mysterious, concept of kundaḷini. The psychophysical space (mandala), which we call an individual, is actually a field for energy to operate. We have seen above how the cakras represent several levels of this energy dynamics. But the source of energy is hidden and inarticulate, and the full potential normally not realized. The vast storehouse of energy in its normal and primal state is pictured as a serpent, asleep with its tail tucked in its mouth, making three coils and a half, and lying right at the entrance of the sushumna, blocking it. Because of its characteristic form, the hidden energy-store is called 'kundalini', meaning 'coiled', like an earring. This form is abandoned only when the energy wakes up and becomes active–a case with none but the great yogins. Normally, it is profoundly asleep all through our lives, and we are not even vaguely aware of its existence. Tantra and Yoga prescribe procedures to arouse it.

This storehouse of energy is linked with the 'root-basic' center of our constitution. Situated, according to one account, two finger-breadths above the anus and two finger-breadths below the genital organ, the 'root-basis' is visualized as a lotus, and in the middle of the lotus is a triangular space, figuratively called womb or vulva (*yoni*), attached to the lower end of the sushumna canal, already described. Inside this triangular space towards the bottom is perched 'the self-born emblem' (*svayambhulinga*), shining like molten gold and facing downward. Above this 'emblem' is the kundalini, "fine as a fibre of the tender lotus stalk, gently blocking the mouth of the susumna door". Although sluggish and asleep, it (or she, because the usual supposition is that kundalini is a goddess) gleams like a chain of bright lights on a dark night. As long as this energy-store is asleep, one is outward oriented (*bahir-mukha*); the subject-object duality persists; the body is heated and cooled alternately so that it is gradually worn out; and man is phenomenally bound. But as soon as it is aroused (*jagarana* or *utthapana*), it becomes tense and stiff like a rod and begins to ascend the susumna tract. On its upward journey, it passes through the six centres, striking against the downward facing petals, and turning them up. This denotes the total transformation of the individual's orientations and attitudes. According to some texts, kundalini pierces the lotuses and burns them up. It is in this sense that kundalini is called 'the mystic fire'.

Of interest in the accounts concerning the action of the aroused kundalini is the view that each center gets animated and illumined as the 'serpent power' passes through it. Besides the mystic import of the energy-store that the kundalini actually is, it is considered to be the place of origin for the vital currents that sustain life (*vayu*), for the seed of life that ramifies into phenomenal involvement (*bindu*), and for the sound that unifies and differentiates (*nada*). These three, responsible for individuality and survival, animation and articulation, function in a passive and constrained manner when the kundalini is sluggish. But they become active and free on kundalini's arousal. It means a reorganization of one's energies and orientations, a restructuring and a revitalization.

There are certain signs (which are by no means all of them pleasant) that suggest that kundalini has been awakened: bodily heat increases, sweating occurs copiously; there are all over the body, sharp sensations like scorpion-bite, and so on. But the urge to continue the exercise is so imperative that after this stage one does not usually give up. As one perseveres, however, these signs give way to more abstract and less distracting signs. It is interesting that these are at first essentially vigorous auditory hallucinations (the expression has been used guardedly), like sounds made by the sea at a distance, peals of thunder, and the roar of the waterfalls. Then the sounds become softer and more pleasant: jingling and tinkling of ornaments worn on the body, the soft strains from a hand-drum, the muffled sound from a hand-bell, the musical notes from a lute or flute. Finally, the sound becomes exceedingly subtle, like the humming of a bee. At this stage, it is reported that one feels dizzy, and salivation becomes copious; the heart-beat gets fainter, but steadier; bodily sensations are benumbed, and immediate surroundings seem to fade away. Later, one begins to hear distinctly the exceedingly subtle sound that is internal, and which emanates from the very essence of the individual. This is 'the voice of inner silence', unstruck, and inarticulate. Simultaneously in some cases, but as frequently reported subsequently, one begins to 'see things': dots of bright light, flames of fire, orb of brilliance, gleaming lines of diverse colours, and geometric patterns of great variety and light. Higher stages are said to be characterized by 'sights' of stars, bright and whirling circles, dense fog and smoke, mirage, tiny dots of dazzling hue between the eye-brows or on the forehead, a steady light from an oil-lamp which no wind disturbs, and great illumination within. It is recognised that such signs (nimittas) are subject to laws of individual differences. They depend considerably, not only on the particular techniques employed for the awakening of kundalini, but on the practitioner's temperament, talent, early experiences and situational involvements, including the master's instructions.

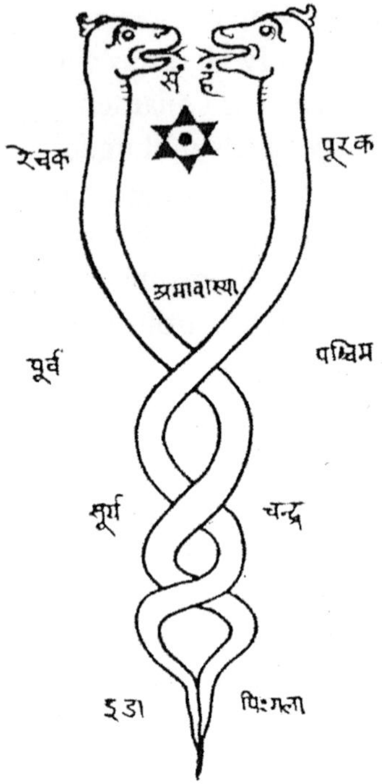

ASCENT OF KUNDALINI making three knots

Besides the six centers, in the upward journey of kundalini, three 'knots' (*granthi*) are also said to be pierced through: the basal knot (at the muladhara center) called "Brahma's knot", the middle knot (at the anahata center) called "Vishnu's knot" , and the top knot (at the ajna center) called "Siva's knot". These are respectively areas of stress concerning emergence, poise and dissolution that are necessarily involved in phenomenal existence. After piercing through the six centers, commingling with the moon's orb that the thousand petals of the highest lotus constitute, causes 'nectar' to ooze out.[26] After reaching its destination, which marks the culmination of the Sadhana, the kundalini returns home (*i.e. muladhara*) by the same path. During its ascent, the individual is reported to experience illumination, and during its descent (or return) it is said to suffuse the individual with profound tranquillity described as ambrosial delight.[27] The lowest center is the home of energy (*Sakti*), while the highest center is the residence of consciousness (*Siva*). Phenomenal life keeps them apart, and hence stresses of all sorts come to the lot of man. Sadhana can bring them together, and the union of the two eliminates all stress and secures the delight of undifferentiated existence. This achievement is styled 'paravrtti' (total transformation), where not only the normal stress-producing conditions disappear but even the ordinary coordinates are transmuted. It is a case of regeneration of the individual, revitalization in one sense and reintegration in another.

Basic to the Tantrik ideology is the conception of life as a configuration of vital currents (*prana*). Sun's energy is said to produce and preserve in all living beings the conditions necessary for life while at the same time burning them up. In man, the solar energy divides itself into ten aspects (or currents); five major (*prana, apana, samana, vyana* and *udana*), and five minor (*naga, kurma, krakara, devadatta* and *dhananjaya*). They support the body, and cause all action. The expression 'prana' signifies ideas of primacy (*pra*) and subtle force (*ana*). Prana is the home of spirit (*jiva*), called picturesquely 'the swan' (hamsa, ham signifying outward flow, and sa inward flow), the mythical bird that constantly moves out of the celestial lake Manasa on the Himalayan heights and back to it. Prana moves along the seven hundred million arteries or nerve channels (*nadis*) that compose the body, although its chief centers are the heart (*hrt*), navel (*nabhi*), nose-tip, and the great toes. As the prana moves along the arteries, consciousness is occasioned as a by-product, as an epiphenomenon. The movement of prana normally is irregular, spasmodic, jerky and strained. This is because of our stimulations, urges, excitement and activity. Therefore, normal consciousness is narrow, stressful and shallow. Most of the Tantrik techniques emphasize that it is not consciousness that should be sought to be corrected, but the basic vital currents that should be handled in order that consciousness spontaneously gets expanded, relaxed and deep. And it is thus that 'control of breath' (*pranayama*) figures prominently in all such techniques.

India has developed an elaborate theory of the breathing process. Breath alternates during the course of the day between the left nostril (connected with ida, representing moon, and in effect cooling) and the right nostril (connected with pingala, representing sun, and in effect warming). Normally, breath passes through the arteries 960 times an hour. From midnight to noon, it flows copiously along the nerves, and from noon to midnight along the blood vessels. Precisely at midnight and noon, it is equal in both systems. At sunrise it ascends through the nerves along with the course of the sun, and towards sunset it descends into the blood vessels. During our normal respiration, inhalation is an active process and exhalation a passive one. Thoughts arise and cease in accordance with the respiratory rate. In an ordinary individual, thoughts are muffled, clouded, sluggish, excited, inadequately articulated; they pass with inordinate speed, or jostle confusedly because his breathing habits are improper. Weather, health, diet, diseases, rest, anxiety, guilt-feelings and cares have an impact not only on the rate of respiration but on the amount of air inhaled and exhaled. If breath does not alternate between the nostrils but continues in one nostril beyond the normal period of an hour and fifty minutes, it is symptomatic of impairment of health due to either excess of heat or of cold. If the breath moves in and out through a single nostril for as long as 24 hours, the derangement of humours is serious; if the condition prevails for two or three days, the illness is serious enough.

The science of pranayama recognises the need to change quickly the flow of breath, to regulate the flow of the vital currents in the arteries, to suspend the breath inhaled, or to keep out the exhaled breath for a definite period. These are in effect techniques to gain mastery over thoughts. The time required for a thought to emerge into awareness is said to be 6/25 of a second; but when inhaled breath is restrained, the time taken for the thought to flash out in awareness would be 12/25 of a second; when the retention is of a longer duration, the thought would require as long as one to one and a half hours. That is to say, the thought is 'fixed' or held out (*dharana*). The thought-arousal is totally suspended if one can restrain the breath inside his body for 13¾ minutes without a flurry. This goes by the name of 'samadhi' (one-pointedness, or settling the mind). The Tantrik texts suggest several devices for 'thoughtlessness' (un-mani or 'no-mind exercises') like the Sambhavi-mudra where the mind is absorbed as a result of gazing intently on the nose-tip or at objectless space, also regulating the breath in the arteries at the same time.

During 24 hours, the number of respirations is calculated by the Yogacudamani-Upanisad to be 21,600 (15 respirations for a minute and 900 for an hour). These are distributed among the seven centers (the seventh being the *manascakra*) as follows: muladhara, 600 respirations taking a total of 40 minutes; svadhisthana, manipura and anahata, each 600 in 6 hours and 40 minutes; visuddha, ajna and manas, each 1000 in one hour, six minutes and 40 seconds.

The breath that is exhaled is believed to be accompanied by the mystic utterance of 'ham' from the very core of one's being, and inhaling of the breath by the syllable 'sa'. When ex-halation-inhalation order is followed, it is termed the 'ascent' and the mystic utterance is "hamsa" (also the word for the mythical swan that lives in the Himalayan heights). When, however, the inhalation-exhalation order is followed, it is the 'descent' and the mystic utterance would be "so' ham" ('I am he', a Vedantic maha-vakya). The prana is looked upon as the mystic fire that leaves the system with 'ham' and enters it with 'sa'; the spirit (jiva) is imagined to be performing passively but ceaselessly the ritual of muttering 'hamsa', which is the nature of the goddess of life ('hamsa-japa' in paropasana).[28] The sound of this mystic muttering is generated at the muladhara and is articulated at the anahata, which in fact is the prime support of the spirit. The purpose of the practices included in the Sadhana of this category is to make this muttering conscious and deliberate, so that the sound rises above the anahata and carries the kundalini along with it.

SAHASRARA-CHAKRA

SVASTIKA-MANDALA, illustrating the arrangement of the universe and the vital currents within the individual.

NADI-MANDALA, illustrating the involvement of Macrocosm in Microcosm

ADEPTS AND ATTITUDES

The Tantra is obviously not attractive to the multitude, because it involves attitudes which are different from, and sometimes contrary to, those which are normally held, and because it requires extraordinary effort. And the Tantra's externals and the superficialities are likely to induce in one an aversion for the discipline as a whole. The Tantra itself recognises this, and therefore, makes the Tantrik practices as little known to others as possible. The secrets are revealed to none but the really serious and the fully ready. Thus, 'initiation' (*diksha* or *abhisheka*) is made an indispensable prerequisite for the practices. The Tantrik initiation is not to be confused with mere 'instruction' (*upadesa*). It is transmission of certain effective doctrines by transforming the recipient entirely. The process involves elaborate and careful preparation where texts and manuals occupy a secondary role, the primary task being the ritualistic involvement with the teacher. It has already been mentioned that the importance given to the teacher in the Tantra is very great. Says a text: "There can be no salvation without initiation, and there can be no initiation without a teacher" ;[29] "For one without initiation there is no progress, nor success; therefore one must by all means get initiated by a teacher".[30] The expression 'diksha' ('initiation') is a compound of two ideas, "to give" or "to endow" divine qualities (*di*), and "to destroy" or "to remove" (ksha) the sins and obstructions, thereby freeing the individual from phenomenal fetters.[31]

One may reasonably expect that the teacher (Guru) will observe and study the novice's defects and distractions, talent and temperament and then decide on the particular initiation that is likely to profit him. For, initiation places not only a profound but direct responsibility on the teacher with regard to his pupil's success in his career. It is a personal transmission of unseen but enormous power from the teacher to the pupil as effectively as possible and as confidentially as feasible. The Tantra emphasises tradition based on such personal communication, and frowns on picking up practices from books and hearsay. It insists that one who gets initiated must guard the details thereof zealously, for mentioning them in public would lead him to unpleasant states of existence.[32]

Initiation means for the individual a total transformation. His whole being is now uprooted from normal moorings, and keyed to a different structure-function. Formally, during initiation the individual is given a new name, and the ritual sequences suggest a rebirth. The initiated is no longer the biological son of his human parents, the member of a profession, or the member of a caste. He has ritualistically given up all former associations, and is thus dead for all practical intents. He is ready to grow-up in a new setting. Initiation is of two types, or operates at two levels : (1) initiation for life, which makes the initiated an altogether different individual, functioning with entirely new coordinates, becoming dead to his old modes of behaviour, old associates and old situations; and (2) initiation for a particular ritual, which is temporary. The latter is frequently known as 'entrance into the circle' (*cakra*). A citation from

Mahanirvana-tantra will make the position clear: "When one enters into the Bhairavi-Cakra, names and castes are lost, conventional inhibitions do not apply. One is exactly like the other. But, on coming out of the circle, each assumes his name and caste again, and each attends to his job as an ordinary work-a-day man".[33] It may be mentioned in passing that the 'cakra' cult in some parts of India degenerated into orgiastic clubs, with obscene and outlandish rites. And this was directly responsible for the disrepute which Tantra fell into.

Initiations differ also according to whether the rituals are external or are merely mental. The Tantra is classified into Kulacara and Samayacara. The former is engaged with external rites and rituals while the latter is characterized by internal worship conducted in ones own 'heart-lotus', without necessarily having to recite the sacred formulae, or to make offerings to fire, or to engage in any worship detail whatever.[34] Samayacara is an interesting contemplative technique where visualizations are all important. In fact, the Vajrayana sadhana, the Buddhist Mahayana thought-practice complex, developed out of this technique. And in this kind of abstract worship, instructions, explanations and guidance from an adept become indispensable and all important. It is, therefore, that Samayacara is said to be learnt directly from the teacher.[35] The novice here retires after instruction by the teacher to a solitary place and practises contemplation alone. The other kind of Tantra is always community-oriented. Practice is done in groups, and there are well-defined rituals available for observation and imitation.

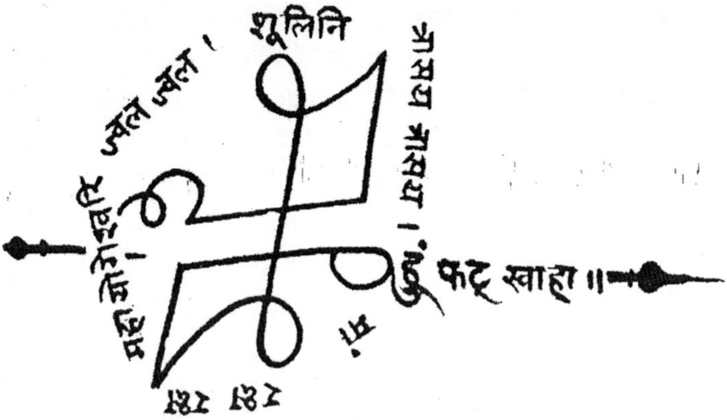

MARIKA-YANTRA against epidemics

In the Tantra, two kinds of 'sacrifices' are recognized: one external (*bahiryaga*), and the other internal (*antaryaga*). It is acknowledged that the latter (performed in *Samayacara*) is the superior one. One indulges in external acts of worship only until wisdom dawns.[36] While external worship is not condemned, it is dubbed as decidedly inferior. However, the need and usefulness of such worship for certain types of men are also suggested. Three types of Tantrik dispositions are mentioned: animal or carnal disposition (*pasu-bhava*), valiant or dynamic disposition (*vira-bhava*) and divine or tranquil disposition (divya-bhava). Under sixteen years, the aspirant is generally ignorant and incapable of understanding right the subtleties of energy-arousal. If, however, he is religiously inclined he spends his time studying scriptures, worshipping deities, and performing the prescribed rituals (albeit mechanically). He leads a disciplined life, without however going to excesses but being earnest about spiritual advancement. Notwithstanding this, his mind is still under-developed, and his feelings and dispositions still immature. This phase of religious life tied to instincts and urges is known as 'animal disposition'. It is no doubt low, but has the capability of passing on to higher stages. When the individual grows older and becomes mature as a result of study, experience or contact with the right teacher, he begins to understand the subtleties, and becomes steadfast in the practice of virtue. His actions reveal courage and conviction. Nothing can frighten him or tempt him off the path he has chosen. He perseveres, endures and pushes on, against all

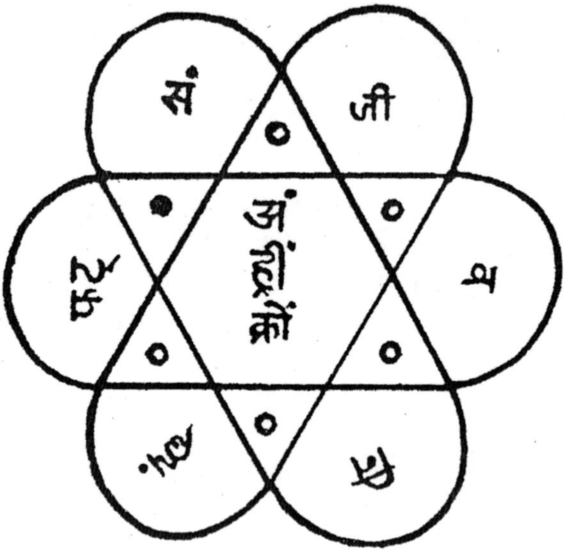

SAMJIVANA-YANTRA used in rituals relating to revival of the dead

odds. He is described as having the 'valiant or dynamic disposition', also termed 'great disposition' (mahabhava). He has conquered his anger, greed, passion, envy and worry; and he has neither inhibitions nor reservations, neither fears nor anxiety while he engages himself even in the rather gruesome experiments like the savasadhana (experiments with a corpse in a crematorium). The next stage is that of 'divine disposition'. Here the practitioner is almost like a god, having abandoned qualities of good and bad, pleasure and pain, right and wrong, and being perfectly tranquil and pure at heart; he is not driven by instincts, nor is he prey to temptations. He has freed himself from phenomenal constraints.

Vamakesvara-tantra defines 'disposition' (*bhava*) as a mental process, a quality of the mind, capable of being handled only at the psychological level.[37] The above classification of disposition into three types is with regard to the mental energy that is brought to bear (*saktipradhan-yat*). And there is a supposition that the physical constitution is also of three types: superior, middling and inferior. The superior is characterised by the dominance of the sattvik element (wisdom), the middling of rajasik element (energetic action), and the inferior of *tamasic* element (Lethargy-ignorance-infatuation). The variety of Tantrik practice that suits and benefits each type of individual must be determined by the master, because successful practice presupposes temperamental facility. One of the texts suggests 'daksina' path for the inferior, 'vama' path for the middling and 'uttara' for the superior.[38] Likewise, for the inferior ('animal disposition') Vedic rituals, worship of gods like Siva and Vishnu are recommended; for the middling ('valiant disposition') the 'siddha' and 'vama' rituals, and for the superior ('divine disposition') only 'kaula' rituals. The classification of personality into three types is elaborated in some of the Tantrik manuals and it is linked with the concept of 'seven-fold conduct' (*saptacara*). After detailing the seven paths, a text sums up: "Many[39] are the paths mentioned by those who are adepts in practice and experts in scriptural lore; but one must follow the path suggested to him by his

AGNI-STAMBHANA-YANTRA for extinguishing fire

The more interesting view, however, is the arrangement of the three 'dispositions' mentioned above in a sequential order. The 'animal disposition' is said to be the primary stage, universal in its scope; "all the animals, as ground for human beings on earth to be founded upon".[41] And it is considered a necessary stage; and everyone, however evolved, must start only here. When wisdom begins to shine, the 'valiant disposition' will set in; and then 'gradually' (*kramena*) one becomes 'divine' in his disposition. The three dispositions are accommodated to the major stages of life: childhood, adulthood and old age. And in some texts, the consecrations (*abhisheka*) are made the turning points of the three dispositions. The normal householder, being initiated into some mantras, starts with the 'animal' stage. He lives according to conventional norms, fulfilling all ritualistic expectations. Then when he obtains the saktabhiseka (consecration as a Tantrik practitioner), he continues to live at home but is indifferent to normal cares and worries of domestic life as well as social participation. He is called a 'householder-recluse' (*grhavadhuta*). When in this condition he advances and gets 'the full consecration' (*purnabhisheka*) the 'valiant' stage starts. He now stays away from home and commences visiting cemeteries for pyre-practice cita-sadhana), crematorium-practice (*smasana-sadhana*), esoteric circle-practices (*cakra-sadhana*), practices with women consorts (yogini-sadhana), and indulges in the five 'm's (wine, fish, flesh, gestures and copulation). The last mentioned practice is esoteric : the articles mentioned

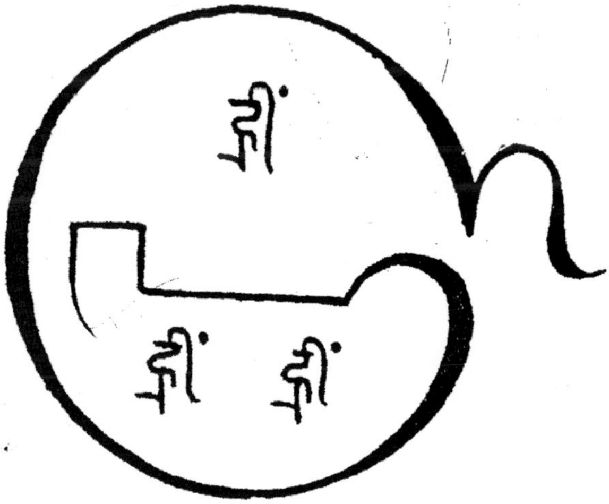

VASIKARA-YANTRA, for eliminating opposition and securing affection

are in fact symbolic and refer to accomplishments in the psychic centres. Unscrupulous masters and uncultured students, together with the forces of ignorance and temptation, have helped to bring infamy on this practice.

The practitioner at this stage also practices the 'six actions' of sorcery and witch-craft : pacification (*santi*), possession (*vasikarana*), hold-up (*stambhana*), rousing enmity (*vidveshana*), driving-away (*uccatana*) and killing (*marana*). After the 'valiant' stage, the practitioner becomes eligible to 'the great-empire consecration' (*mahasamrajyadiksha*). But this means giving up all worldly involvement and devoting oneself entirely to the yogic attainment of Brahman. He is now on the last lap of his pilgrimage. His disposition is naturally 'divine'; he is now above the human frailties and beyond the agitations that plague the common folk or the early aspirant.

THE IDEOLOGICAL BASIS

The Tantra is primarily a practical discipline and its philosophy was never crystallized. The need was never strongly felt and much of the instruction was oral and situational. Some of the Tantrik texts, like Saradatilaka, do deal with philosophical matters, but these accounts are neither systematic nor consistent. It is hard, therefore, to define and describe what may be called the Tantrik philosophy. The working presuppositions of the Saiva, Vaisnava, Sakta and the so-called Buddhist Tantras appear different; and the functional role of the concepts in each Tantra seems to vary. The common idea, however, is that of 'energy' (*sakti*), which is a sort of Tantrik counterpart of the Vedantic maya and the Samkhyan prakrti.[42] The Tantrik tradition being theistic, they point to the supreme and absolute but qualified Lord (*saguna-paramesvara*), whom some Tantrik texts describe as "glorious with being, sentience and bliss' (*saccidanandavibhava*). In Him is inseparably merged the infinite and transcendental energy (*sakti*) as His aspect (*kala*), which is beyond the phenomenal context. But the Lord by His free will sets energy into motion, and brings forth creations as oil is pressed from the oil-seeds.[43] Creation is merely the manifestation of energy, and the texts illustrate the process by drawing a parallel to the arousal (or rather revival) of remembrance in a person who wakes up from deep sleep. His memory which had merged in him, lost as it were, reappears as soon as wakeful awareness is established. There is conjured 'a vision of void' as a result of which emerges the undifferentiated and diffuse light sound nucleus (*para-nada*), 'filling the void.' This void-essence focuses itself and crystallizes into the 'transcendental drop' (*para-bindu*), which is a sort of materialization of the Lord's 'action-energy' (*kriya-sakti*). This 'drop', being creative, structures itself into two categories : 'the phenomenal drop' (apara-bindu), highlighting the aspect of self-awareness in the Lord (the Siva category) and 'the seed' (*bija*) of all creation, emphasizing the energy aspect of the Lord (the sakti category). This splitting is accompanied by a secondary light-sound complex (*apara-nada*), which is described as 'the great sound' or 'the sound-absolute' (*mahanada* or *sabdabrahma*). In fact, this light-sound complex is what holds the two categories together and thus symbolizes their union.

The thought-transference from macrocosmic level to the microcosmic led the Tantra to find in man the counterpart of this 'great sound' in 'the coiled serpent' (*kundalini*). It is the causal energy in man (*sakti*), represented by a triangle consisting of the three categories mentioned above as its sides: 'the drop' (*bindu*), 'the seed' (*bija*), and 'the sound' (*nada*), all emerging from the materialized 'transcendental drop' (*para-bindu*). Even as the entire creation issues from the 'sound-absolute', man's being and behaviour arise out of the 'coiled serpent-power'. It is 'coiled' in the sense of being inactive normally; it rests in itself, perfectly self-contained, turned on itself and devoid of all outward orientation. The secondary 'light-sound complex' (*apara-nada*) or 'the great sound', located in between the eyebrows, is imagined to enter the central psychic canal, sushumna, and flow down to the 'basal center' (*muladhara*) and rest there in the form of kundalini.

The purpose of Tantrik sadhana is to rouse this slumbering giant, who when roused would return to the psychic center between the eyebrows ascending along the sushumna canal. Kundalini in its initial wakefulness is described as 'visarga' ('sending forth') 'discharge', 'departure'; the latter is also the mark of hard aspiration after the modifier in the Sanskrit alphabet. It is represented (as in the alphabet) by two dots one placed on top of the other. The dot on the top is identified with 'fire' (agni) while the one below with 'moon' (*soma*). We have seen above that this symbolizes male-female configuration (or biunity). The aspirate mark has no doubt two components, but it is not indicative of duality. It points out rather to the fact that these two are the necessary structural elements involved in a unity; each divorced from the other would be meaningless. In the Tantrik texts, this stage of initial but incipient activity on the part of the awakened energy is styled 'awareness-instant' (*cit-kala*), which booms and buzzes, and develops into a pleasurable prospect of activity (technically described as 'bliss', ananda). Carrying the sound-imagery further, kundalini is said to comprise of all audible (*akshara*) and visible (*varna*) sound; and the first flush of awareness is the initial sound-form 'a', from which in due course the entire alphabet proceeds. This 'awareness-sound' as it arises in the 'root-basic' center is termed the 'transcendental speech' (*para-vak*), characterized by mere intention or will (*kama*) which is unspecified but fundamental. It is not a desire for something or a will to do anything; but the glimmer of volition which lies at the back of all life. In fact, we read in the Tantrik accounts that life proceeds only from this intention or will. Life (*prana*) is the phenomenal counterpart and an emergent of the transcendental 'awareness instant'. If the former is symbolized by 'a', the first letter of the alphabet the latter as the final effect is symbolized by 'ha', the last letter; it is also pictured as a swan (*hamsa*). 'Aha' thus represents the totality of origin and effect, of the transcendental and the phenomenal, of awareness and activity; 'parama-hamsa' is a word that denotes 'the whole man' in whom the elements are perfectly integrated.

The Saivite Tantra looks upon '*a*' as Siva (pure awareness or illumination, *prakasa*), the absolute being; and 'ha' is sakti (the energy aspect thereof, or the inherent expressive activity *vimarsa*), the phenomenal emergence.[44] The two are paralleled by Brahman and Maya in Advaita Vedanta. The coming together of the two categories (the union being symbolized by the terminal 'm') is signified by the Sanskrit expression 'a-ham' ('I' or ego), which also comprehends in itself the entire alphabet. The mass of this union is technically termed 'mithuna-pinda' (the pair-body, or two-in-one), or 'Siva-Sakti' (awareness-energy).[45] When 'awareness' and 'activity' thus unite in the act of 'visarga' the unity is spoken of as 'kama-kala' (aspects of desire). 'Awareness (*prakasa*), when implicit in 'activity' (*vimarsa*), is represented by a white coloured 'drop', symbolic of semen or male energy; 'activity' as implicit in 'awareness' is symbolized by a red coloured 'drop', also called 'sound' (*nada*), denoting female energy. The two drops really are two aspects of the 'transcendental drop' but in its phenomenal phase (called Kama, the aspects of which are the two coloured 'drops'). 'Awareness' is likened to fire, and activity' to the butter which melts in its heat, And interaction between the two is described as 'bliss' (*ananda or hardhakala*).

The 'transcendental drop' is the kundalini in its original condition, altogether uninvolved in individuation and unrelated altogether to the phenomenal evocations. In this condition it is called 'mahamaya'. But when 'awareness-activity' arises in it, the pristine state of quiet is disturbed and it becomes individuated, and bound to phenomenal conditions.[46] This is the 'coiled serpent-power' that the Tantra seeks to handle. In the normal individual, however, the free power of activity lies hidden or is in a dissolved state within 'awareness' (*antarlina-vimarsa*). This condition is what is described as 'coiled'; kundalini is said to be asleep here. And in such a condition, 'awareness' is important and inert (Siva is here figured as sava, a corpse). When owing to the Tantrik practices 'the power' stirs up, then 'I-ness' (*ahamta*) or egoity is instituted. In this context, egoity means merely 'self-awareness', the individuated power discovering its own identity. As against it, there is projection of the same power onto the phenomenal canvas; and consequently there appears the external world of things and events. The source of this externalization is spoken of as 'non-egoity' (*anaham*). When 'self-awareness' interacts with the projected phenomenal world, we have the relating process, 'thisness' (*idamta*).

The Natha tradition takes the same stand but elaborates on individual development. The abstract world as projected by the awareness-energy complex out of an initial stir (*spanda*) of inspiration (*sphurti*) is described as the 'transcendental structure' (*parapinda*), a materialization that is cosmic in its import. But as individuated with the nucleus of 'egoity', it becomes transactional, and it is termed 'individual structure' (*vyashti-pinda*). In each individual, however, the transcendental structure is reflected. The entire universe is contained within one's body.[48] The awareness-energy complex occurs in the individual as spirit and body : the spirit is Siva and the body is Sakti. The dichotomy in our thought and action is unnatural and therefore stressful. The goal of the Natha practitioner is to realize in one's own being the identity of Siva and Sakti, to integrate the two apparently divergent dimensions, and to perceive the entire universe as the expression of Siva-Sakti. The Natha practice suggests a procedure which is both natural (*sahaja*) and effective for transmuting the body into the spirit[49], thereby achieving enduring and unbroken inner identity. This procedure is called 'harmonizing' (*samarasa*) the immanent, the transcendent and the universal into one reality. Our ordinary consciousness is fragmented, torn into states and conditions and processes, and therefore our identity is involved in a crisis. The 'splitting' causes pain because of its unnaturalness, and ego involvement in each detail frustrates the basic self-awareness (*ahamta*). The Yogi, like a Taoist, recommends a perfectly natural and therefore relaxed and easy life; the mind should become 'sky-like' (*kha-sama*), freed from all specific fixations.

SOURCE MATERIAL

Considering the anxiety displayed by the Tantrik adherents to keep their lore a well-guarded secret, it is surprising that we have a very large number of Tantrik works, most of them well preserved in public institutions (like royal libraries) and not a few of them given rather wide publicity. The extent of Tantrik literature is vast, and the content various, so various in fact that an adequate classification is almost impossible. Besides, most of the Tantras that we possess are indefinite about their philosophical positions, sectarian affiliations and authorship. Not a few of them are rambling in their accounts and grandiose in their claims. And many of them are obviously late compositions, the dates extending from the 10th to the 18th century. Themes overlap, ideas are repeated and verses are reproduced in the Tantrik works so much that it is difficult to determine borrowals.

There are, however, some criteria for classifying the Tantrik texts that appear to be rather old. One of them is based on the 'amnaya' concept: (1) works of eastern 'amnaya' (predominently belonging to the mantra path); (2) works of the western 'amnaya' (karma path); (3) works of the northern 'amnaya' (jnana path); (4) works of the southern 'amnaya' (bhakti path); and (5) works of the central 'amnaya' (comprehensive or mixed). Another is based on the 'guna' idea: (a) the texts emphasizing sattvik nature (the Tantra proper); (2) those which are rajasik in nature (*e.g.*, the yamalas); and (3) those which are tamasik (*e.g.*, the damaras). Still another relies on geographical areas of prevalence: Gauda (Bengal and neighbourhood), Kashmira (and the frontier areas like the Swat valley, called in the old texts Uddiyana) and Kerala (South India). It appears that this was a widely accepted classification of traditions (sampradaya). There is a classification based on whether the texts follow Vedic religion (*veda-marga*), Buddhism, or Jainism. There are some Tantrik texts that advocate secrecy (vamacara), others that do not mind publicity (daksina-cara), and still others that are 'mixed' (misra), *i.e.*, following vamacara in secret and daksinacara in public.

Although the Tantra is mostly an approach to Sakti and therefore properly described as Sakta, there are Tantrik texts purporting to extol Siva or Visnu. Accordingly, they are designated Saiva or Vaisnava Tantras. The Saiva Tantra includes pure Saiva, Pasupata, Kalagamana and Kapalika. The Tantrik works of the Saiva persuasion are traditionally twenty-eight in number while those of the Vaisnava are 108. The former (also called Saiva-agama) are again grouped into two categories: Saiva proper (10 works like Kamikagama, Karanagama, Suprabhedagama and Ajita-gama), and Raudra (18 works like Vijayagama, Nihsvasagama. Kiranagama, Svayambhuvagama and Rauravagama). The Vaishnava works are principally grouped under Vaikhanasa (like the Samhitas of Marici, Bhrgu, Atri and Kasyapa). Pancaratra (like *Jayakhya-samhita, Pushkara-samhita* and *Satvata-samhita*), and Tantra-sara (followed by Madhva devotees).

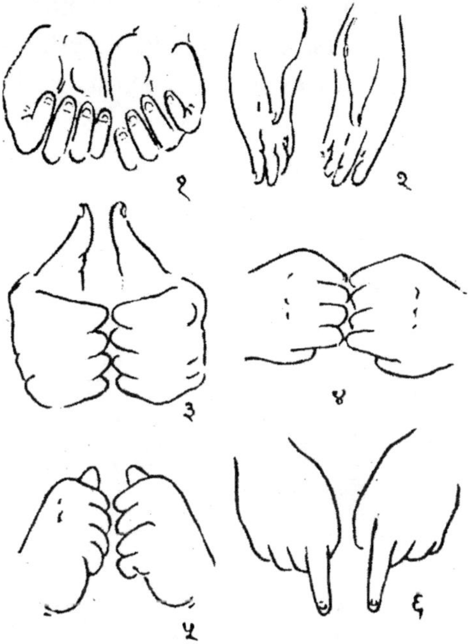

१. आवाहन २. स्थापन ३. संनिधापन ४. संरोधन ५. सम्मुखीकरण
६. अवकुण्ठन

SOME MUDRAS USED IN WORSHIP

The Saktas are either Kaulas or Samayacarins, while the differences between them are numerous and rather vague, we may roughly describe the former as given to external rituals while the latter as preferring 'internal worship' (*antaryaga*). The Kaulas are worshippers of Kali,[50] and maintain secrecy in their rituals.[51] And their rituals are said to include drinking wine, eating meat and fish, hand-gestures and sexual indulgence (the five 'm's). But they also insist that the Kaula path is not for one who lacks control over his impulses and senses.[52] There are several Kaula sects like 'purvakula' (who take the five 'm's only symbolically), 'Uttarakula', 'Kapalika', and 'Digambara' (all of whom seem to resort to outlandish rituals). They all identify themselves with Bhairava and worship in a nude state the Goddess.[53] The Kaulas are said to assume numerous garbs: they are Saktas (or *Kaulas*) within, but Saivas in appearance, and pass for Vaisnavas in assemblies.[54] The Samayacarins, on the other hand, are more restrained in their ideas and practices; they are given to symbolic Sricakra worship and their philosophy is based on the 'centers' in the body. They have a five-fold canon named after the Vedic sages, Vasishtha, Sanaka, Suka, Sanandana and Sanatkumara.

KALI YANTRA, used in the Worship of the Mother Goddess

Most of the Tantrik ideas got crystallized at the hands of the Siddhas and the Nathas, who lived during the early centuries of the Christian era. The Apabhramsa dohas and the Caryagitis of the Siddhas and the Sanskrit works of the

Nathas (especially *Gorakshanatha*) are important sources of Tantrik ideas. Under the impact of the Siddhas and the Nathas, a rich Tantrik literature sprang up during the medieval ages. Kashmir Saivism and South Indian Saiva Siddhanta have very interesting works bearing on Tantra. Kashmir Saivism is well represented by Somananda's Sivadrshti, Abhinavagupta's Tantraloka and Tantrasara, and Kshemaraja's Pratyabhijna-hrdaya and Spandasandoha. Saiva Siddhanta treatises are all in Tamil. Important among them are Manikka-vacakar's Tiruvacakam, Meykandadevar's Sivajnanabodam, Sakalagamapandita's Sivajnanasiddhiyar, and the writings of Tirujnana-sambandar. Appar and Sundarar made important contributions towards crystallizing Tamil Saivism.

The Tantra drew both Jainism and Buddhism within its fold in thc carly centuries of the Christian era. In both these religions, worship of gods and goddesses in the form of Yakshas and Yakshis and adoration of teachers (like tirthankaras, dhyanibuddhas and bodhisattvas) became important involvements. In Jainism, each of the twenty-four Tirthankaras (the ford-making Jinas) came to possess his own characteristic Yaksha and Yakshini. Most of these spirits and divinities were directly borrowed from the folk cults (like Garuda, Kubera, Gomedha, Kimnara, Brahma, Vara-Nandi, Gomukha and Tumburu); some of them were already well-known in Tantrik circles (like Kalika, Vajrasrnkhala, Bhrkuti, Gauri, Jvalamalini and Mahamanasi). It is small wonder that what appealed to popular fancy was the cult of these Tantrik divinities, and therefore numerous Jain Tantrik manuals came to be composed by celebrated Jaina saints. Bhairava-Padmavati-kalpa, Jvala-malini-kalpa, Rshiman-dala-mantra-kalpa, Jagatsudari-prayoga-mala, Sri-chinta-mani-kalpa-sara and Vidhi-prapa are good illustrations of what may be called Jaina Tantra. The Buddhist development in the Tantrik framework forms the subject matter of another volume by me and therefore little about it needs to be said here.

A large proportion of extant Tantrik works is still in manuscripts. Of those that have been printed, many belong to the Kaula and Samaya persuasions. Kubjika-tantra, Saura-samhita, Kirana-tantra, Jayakhya-samhita, Paramesvari-tantra, Kularnava, Maha-nirvana-tantra, Bhavacudamani, Mundamala-tantra, Prayogasara, Kamikagama, Jayasimha-kalpadruma, Jnanasankalini-tantra, Vamakesvara-tantra, Srikrama-tantra, Tantraraja-tantra, Kaulava-linirmaya, Sakti-sangama-tantra, Rudrayamala, Sarada-tilaka, Parananda-sutra, Parasuramakalpa-sutra, Kaula-rahasya, Matanga-paramesvari-tantra (with Ramakantha's comm.), Bhairava-damara, and Kakacandesvara-mata are some of the better known texts. Most of them are still in their Sanskrit original. John Woodroffe (Arthur Avalon) has done much not only to translate some Tantrik works, but to expound the concepts involved in them. Chinta-haran Chakravarti, Haraprasad Sastri, Bhavtosh Bhattacharya, M.P. Pandit, Kapali Sastri, Prabodha Chandra Bagchi, M. Eliade, G. Tucci, P.H. Pott, Gopinath Kaviraj and Hazariprasad Dvivedi are some of the scholars whose writings have illumined many a dark niche in the Tantrik mansion.

Of the numerous Tantrik works that are still in manuscript stage and are included in catalogues, a large number deal with rituals connected with particular deities (like Kurukulla-patala, Ekajata-sadhana, Kumari-tantra, Gauri-yamala, Taranigama, Tarini-nirnaya, Bhairavi-yamala, Matangi-tantra, Varahi-tantra, Lakshmi-kularnava, Bhuta-damara and Mallari-mahatmya); and some are general works (like Tantra-dipika, Tantradarsa, Tantrika-darpana, Prayoga-sara, Brhat-tantra-sara, Saktagama-sarvasva, Mantra-tantra-prakasa, and Nigama-kalpadruma). Some contain the view points of particular sages or schools (like Pippalada-mata, Pingala-mata, Kaulesakoti-prabheda, Goraksha-mahartha-manjari, Dattatreya-samhita, Pherutantra, Vaisampayana-samhita. Soma-sambhu-siddhanta, Gauda-pada-Sakti-sutra and Vidyananda-nibhandha). Some deal with magical rites (like Abhicara-kavaca, Yonitantra, Shat-karma-dipika and Sautramani-tantra), and some are simple worship manuals (like Lingarcana, Pujasara, Krshnar-cana-candrika, Kadi-mata, Kali-kalpa, Sri-cakra-krama and Syama-saparya-krama). Some are in the nature of lexicons and glossaries (like Matrka-kosa, Sanketa-paddhati, Matrkarnave, Mudra-nighantu, Gudhartha-dipika, and Keraliya-*yantra*-sastra. Some describe regional Cults (like Kamarupa-dipika, Kamakhya-tantra Cinatantra, Jayadratha-yamala, Munda-mala-tantra, and Bala-vilasa). Maha-cina-tantra, Rudra-yamala, Tara-tantra, Svatantra-tantra, Nila-sarasvati-tantra indicate Tibetan and Chinese influence on some of the Indian cults. There are Tantras (like Maha-nirvana, Sakti-samgama, Munda-mala, Shatkarma and Maha-cinacara) that recommend aggressive and erotic measures, and there are those (like Kularnava, Parananda and Sri-krama) that insist on austerity. There is an interesting work on mystic diagrams by Damodara, Yantra-cintamani, which claims to be a summary of Atharva-Veda. Of minor, but popular short works must be mentioned Saundarya-Lahari, ascribed to the great Samkara and commented upon by Lolla-Lakshmidhara (about 1500), Bhavanopanishad deemed as an Upanishad and commented upon by Bhaskararaya (1733), Devi-pancastavi, and Nityashodasi-karnava which belongs to Vamakesvara-tantra, Lalitasahasra-nama (with Bhaskara-raya's gloss) and Varivasya-rahasya.

MUKTI-MANDARA used in rituals for achieving liberation

The Tantra literature is thus not only vast but varied. It not only reflects the diversity of outlooks and attitudes, but explains the multiplicity of cults that prevail in our country. It holds the key to understand right the peculiarly incongruous but eminently effective pattern that is called Hinduism.

ANOTHER ANGLE

Twofold is the orientation of consciousness: outward, towards the world; and inward, towards one's own self. The former involves transaction with objects and events in space and time, and is punctuated with experiences.

Perception, sensation, recollection, anticipation, imagination are illustrations of the world-oriented consciousness. The self-oriented consciousness is not so apparent although it is more continuous: it does not cease even in sleep. Normally, it occurs as a passive background for the world-oriented consciousness. The ego-feeling in our attitudes and actions, the subjectivity in the behavioural modes, the deep anguish in frustrating situations and the pleasurable emotions in satisfying situations, all suggest a groundwork of self and its awareness.

The outward orientation is governed by facts of the outer world to a large extent, by the passive sense-receptions occasioned by the presence of, and contact with, these facts. The inward consciousness is normally but a continuation or extension of this outward consciousness: the sense-impressions engender conceptions and feelings as numerous as the facts, and more so because of the mind's ability to construct and create.

The facts are the outer bund and ideas (including sensations and feelings) the inner bund of phenomenon of consciousness in the individual. It does not go beyond the facts in the outward direction and the ideas in the inward direction. Consciousness is characterised by this framework; what we call normal, natural or spontaneous consciousness moves between the facts in the world and ideas in the head. The facts are introjected and the ideas are projected, and this transaction is the essential process of experience.

Indian religions, principally Yoga and Tantra, recognise that this transactional consciousness is but a level, and that there are other levels both beyond the facts in the outward direction and beyond the ideas in the inward direction. Establishment of mind's control over matter, divination of occurrence in the future, materializations and such phenomena figure largely in the treatment of consciousness-levels beyond the facts of the world.

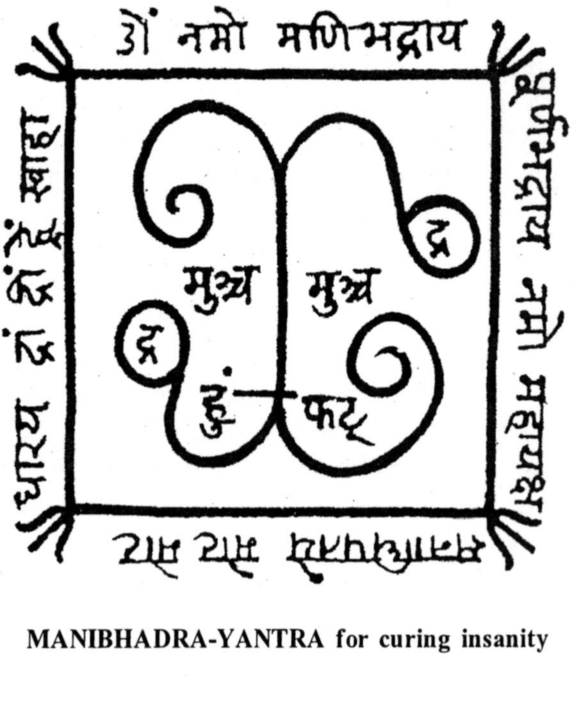

MANIBHADRA-YANTRA for curing insanity

However, Yoga and Tantra are not directly concerned with this aspect of the problem, although both in India and outside they are commonly mistaken for magic and everything that is associated with it. A Yogi or a Tantrik adept is commonly, though erroneously, recognised by the superhuman powers that he possesses, or claims to possess. Yoga and Tantra are primarily concerned with the inward slant: a Yogi is constantly preoccupied with levels of consciousness deeper than ideas and feelings. His is an adventure into the interior; his achievements are all internal, hidden from the common gaze; and, for the same reason, hard to understand or appreciate.

But luckily for the Yogi or the Tantrik it usually happens that the depths are matched by the heights; his achievements of inner levels of consciousness are balanced by an involuntary mastery over material phenomena. The shoot of a plant rises as high in the air as the roots go down in the soil.

When the Upanishad speaks of "the many inner mansions" or the Buddha of "the worlds within man", the reference is to the deeper and hidden levels of consciousness. The need to recognise these levels was felt in the wake of the recognition that the transactional level is unsatisfactory, unstable and far from being final. This level of consciousness being world-bound, is rather passive.

The facts of the world stimulate, and the individual's response is guided by the sense-impressions and the mind. The individual has little control over the sense-function or over the mind, and much less over the facts outside him. His action is non-deliberate, involuntary and almost inescapable. The Indian word for this world-bound consciousness is samsara. This word emphasises the transitional and transitory character of the phenomena involving the individual: consciousness goes round and round the self-same fads and never gets beyond them; it gets stuck at the level of ideas and feelings, and never goes deeper than that. Boredom, misery, frustration, anxiety, tension and stress mark the individual who is thus bound inextricably to the facts over which he has no control.

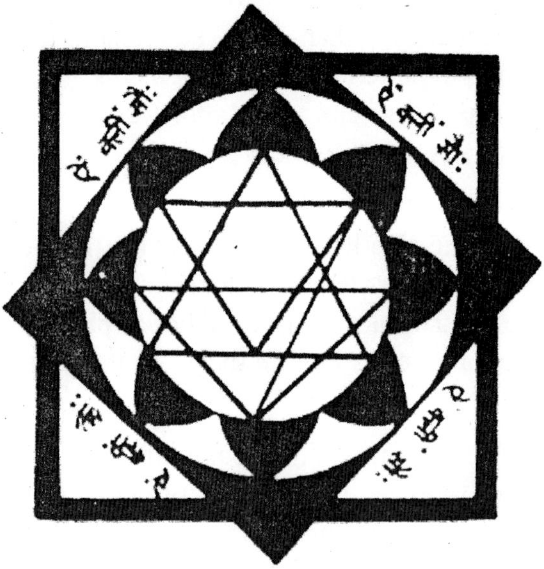

BALA-YANTRA for accomplishment of learning and art

The Indian books describe the state of mind of a man who has been obliged to ride a tiger all the time. He dare not get off its back, lest it should pounce on him. Anxious and tense, frightened and restless, he should ride the tiger without a break! The world-bound consciousness works under a similar necessity. The purpose of all religious exercises, Hindu, Buddhist and Jain, is to enable the individual escape this necessity, to free the consciousness from the bondage with facts, and help it to get into deeper and therefore freer levels. This release from the world's imposition is called Moksha. It does not mean that on obtaining this release the individual merely ceases to exist; nor does it mean that he stops transacting with facts. Yoga, Tantra and Zen insist that a released individual would participate in the world with good cheer, greater strength and indeed with a better perspective. The Vedanta and Tantra call this state of free participation jivanmukti (release while still alive); the old Buddhist books call it saupadisesa-nibbana (extinction while being existent).

Unfortunately, excessive theorising has robbed these expressions of their true psychodynamic import. These words are often held out as equivalent of salvation, or of residence in some heavenly abode after death, divorced from the phenomenal world altogether. This is a wrong interpretation. Yoga and Tantra have strictly no use for after-life; they are for this life and in this world. The Buddha described his doctrine as 'relevant to the present life' (*sanditthiko*), not removed in time (*akaliko*), *viz.* here and now. The 'release' is meaningful only in actual experience, and only in relation to consciousness.

The urge to get released from tension and oppression may arise from one's inability to cope with the demands of existence, or from one's dissatisfaction, intellectual or emotional, with the existing state of affairs. The increased popularity of the psychedelic drugs like Marihuana among youngsters is to be traced to this felt discontent. Marihuana, being euphoric, is said to release the confines of consciousness and bring on a pleasant, friendly, generous, convivial and tolerant attitude, free from inhibitions.

Groups of Indian ascetics have experimented with several preparations from cannabis, like Bhang, Ramrasa, Charas, Ganja and Hashish for the purpose of widening the field of consciousness and reducing the severity of the bondage with facts. It is reported that under the influence of these drugs, inhibitions disappear, conflicts cease, pleasurable sensations increase and the subject becomes more friendly and less critical. More important than these symptoms is the inclination to withdraw from preoccupation with facts; this detachment facilitates introversion and a concern to deepen the levels of consciousness. Studies conducted on Marihuana, LSD, Mescaline and other drugs reveal a similar effect.

No one, however, would seriously consider the employment of these drugs to bring about lasting alteration in the levels of consciousness, to eliminate once and for all the limitations and irritations attending on the transactional consciousness. The effects of drugs are by no means lasting, and an increase in dosage is likely to result in anxiety, guilt-feeling, dejection and restlessness. The drugs are physical agents operating only at the level of transactional consciousness, and are in reality confined to subjective facts and their experiences. It is true that they provide us with peeping holes to observe deeper levels of consciousness and have a direct acquaintance with them; but they do not extend the transactional consciousness nor break through its confines. So long as the drug is active, it may even be that the opacity of the walls that hold the normal transactional consciousness may considerably be lightened. One might feel as if he is in a glass cage, his view unobstructed. But he is in a cage all the same, he cannot reach outside.

Consciousness itself does not get transformed under the impact of the psychedelic drugs, it is the ego-involvement, or "the identification with the ideas" (Patanjali, 1.4), that undergoes change. This is not a positive gain, inasmuch as the ego is after all a small part of the psychic existence, much like the visible top of the iceberg. Transformation does not occur in the foundations: the therapy offered for the misery of existence is little more than symptomatic.

This is the reason why Yoga and Tantra reject drugs as reliable instruments for altering the levels of consciousness. They seek to effect the change at a deeper level, and work with the very springs of one's own being. They do not believe in short-cuts or snappy cures; but insist, on the other hand, on "persistent effort towards steadiness" and "systematic rejection of involvement with facts" (Patanjali, 1-13,15). Buddhism agrees that it is a long-drawn and difficult course involving diligent effort that leads to enlightenment. The final instruction of the Buddha was: "Achieve without slackening your effort" (*appamadena sampadetha*). Zen, which believes in sudden illumination, nevertheless recognises the need for preparatory discipline (Zazen).

It is, therefore, not drugs but discipline that the Indian religions hold out as the aid for altering the levels of consciousness, so that the individual no longer "becomes" and is bound up in the transactional level. The goal of Indian religious practices is to escape this becoming (bhava), to tear up the bonds and to reach a stage from where "there is no return". When the Buddha claimed that it was for him the final birth (antima jati), that there was no more becoming for him, and that he had "cooled down completely" (*sitibhuto*), he meant that he had successfully freed himself from the consciousness that is bound to facts and ideas. He was no longer obliged to operate at the transactional level; he had acquired the facility to go down at will to other levels of consciousness. He could truly say: "That is not mine of which they speak; they are not I of which they tell."[55]

The Buddha's description of consciousness that is not bound to facts and ideas is revealing: "Thus consciousness, being without standing place, is without increase and without individuality; and is liberated. Then it is stable and happy, not agitated and so attains complete peace in itself."[56] Before his times, the Upanishad had described this state in a similar vein: "The knots of the heart are snapped, all doubts that agitate are cut asunder, all obligations disappear when one beholds the beyond."[57] Yoga, Tantra and Buddhist discipline alike seek to bring about this experience into existence, not as an occasional occurrence, but as a stable continuum.

The preparatory discipline suggested by Yoga and Tantra takes the form of withdrawals, rejections and restraints. The purpose is to disabuse the sense-organs and mind from their habitual preoccupation with facts and ideas, and thereby break the apparent solidity of the transactional consciousness. An Upanishad says: "It was the self-existent consciousness that pierced the sense-openings, and therefore it looks out not within. But some bold man, desirous of stability, looked within and discovered the self."[58] The initial discipline thus seeks to plug the openings that make consciousness outward-oriented. It is the nature of consciousness to flow (it is likened to a stream), and when it is stopped in its onward course in the direction of objects and acts in the world, it turns naturally to the ideas. This is a necessary condition, a foothold (*padaniya*) for exploring other and deeper levels of consciousness.

Zen tries to achieve the same result by shocking, by "an abrupt breakthrough." The mind is suddenly thrown out of shape unawares, and in its struggle to regain its balance a momentous transformation comes to pass: other levels within and other fields beyond flash out vividly. Before this can occur, how-ever, an unremitting cultivation of inwardness is indispensable.

The distinction between "the sudden" (*Rinzai*) and the "gradual" (Soto) disciplines is not an absolute one. The "entrance" is made "at one stroke" , but the journey is a long one, a gradual one. The preparation for journey in Zen is not very different in essence from that in Yoga, Tantra or in old Buddhism. Zen also teaches: "Throw away the body to find the spirit." But this does not mean rejection of the world or extreme asceticism, for Zen encourages active participation with the world. What is meant here is pricking the bubble of transactional consciousness.

Dhyana (Pali Jhana, Chinese Ch' an, Japanese Zen) is the technique adopted by all Indian religions for transforming normal consciousness into an extraordinary one. The Sanskrit word means meditation, mindfulness, trance, contemplation, deep introspection, concentration. It is essentially an exertion to focus attention on an inward object. Operationally, it signifies consciousness turning on itself. An Upanishad explains that the purpose is "to make the one form manifold in their own souls."[59] What is apprehended merely as object-awareness is now broken up into its constituent factors including recipient awareness adverting to the object, attention, image-formation and retention. Transactional consciousness is analysed into its inward aspect and outward aspects; and the inward aspect is subjected to the further constructive analysis.

The time-honoured technique of getting used to this inner work is to focus attention on the breathing process. Breath is internal so far as the physical constitution is concerned, but it is external to consciousness. Yoga classifies it under bodily phenomena, and advises watching it and regulating it before further inner work is attempted. The Buddhist meditation known as anapana-sati (mindfulness in breathing- in and breathing-out) suggests careful, analytic and un-involved observation of the phenomenon without, however consciously attempting to regulate it.

The reason for this importance attached to breathing is that it is the only bridge between the outer world and the inner consciousness: besides mind by its very nature closely follows it. Ernst Wood wrote: "There is a certain calmness of mind which reflects itself in rather slow and measured breathing."

Even the bare watching of the breath in the Buddhist anapana-sati, meditation by 'counting', 'following', 'gate-watching', and other stages described in detail by Buddhaghosa[60] brings about an involuntary control of all the physical processes associated with consciousness so that further exploration of levels beyond the transactional level is facilitated. The preliminary exertion helps the development of 'proximity' (*upacara*) which in its turn brings about 'absorption' (*appana*) or trance.

The banishment of external stimuli makes consciousness alert to inner processes; images, conceptions and symbols are high-lighted here. By persevering, these inner processes are stripped of their conventional meanings and properties, and become less objective. This level of consciousness is called in Buddhist books upacara. Consciousness in this stage is expanded, being no longer 'hooked' to facts as in the transactional level. There may be sensory awareness, as when one is watching the nostrils while breathing, or watching the contact of foot with the earth in the cankama-meditation; but the objectivity of stimulations is eliminated and sense-signals are turned off. The glare of reality is no longer there.

Consciousness in this stage, first Jhana (*trance*), appears as an even flow independent of objects. The meditation-manuals compare it with "the spreading of wings when the bird is about to fly" and "the turning round of bees on top of the lotus flower". There is a thrill (*sampahassana*) emanating from the awareness of this consciousness: pleasurable sensations (*sukha*) euphoria (*piti*) and relaxation (*upekkha*) are said to be the attendant feelings.

The physical sensations and feelings which overwhelm this state are eliminated in the second Jhana. Here the experience is entirely subjective and psychological. The pleasurable sensations, euphoria and relaxation increase, but the attainment of inward calmness (*sampasadana*) characterises this level of consciousness, The pleasurable sensations and euphoria are only mildly disturbing, and relaxation gains emphasis.

The third Jhana finds pleasure and euphoria altogether inoperative, although existent. Consciousness in this level is entirely relaxed and perfectly calm (*sukhavihari*). The external stimuli, sense-impressions, ideas and their configurations do not distract the consciousness in this "trance", although the subject is awake and alert. It is what may be called "the level of minimal consciousness.

It may be noted in passing that the effect of drugs, although similar in some details, is altogether different. For instance the New York Mayor's Committee on Marihuana found that "Mari-huana does not change the basic personality structure of the individual. It lessens inhibition and brings out what is latent in his thoughts and emotions but it does not evoke responses which would otherwise be totally alien to him," Similarity consists in the intense subjective feelings of awareness, euphoria (a rich, lively internal experience) and what Walter de la Mare described as 'an extravagant sense of isolation', But these are not transient in the case of trance states described above; nor do the other symptoms like sensory hyperesthesia, distortion of time and space sense, excitement, loss of judgement, ecstasy and aggression common to drugs occur in meditation.

It is true that in early stages of trance experience hallucinations occur, somewhat as they do in the case of LSD, Mescaline and Psilocybin; it is also true that in anapanasati and pranayama the wave-like aspect of the experience comes to pass as in several hallucinogens but depersonalization or "double consciousness", synesthesia, anxiety or paranoid reactions are not involved.

In fact, the symptoms that are associated with the trances mentioned above are looked upon as hindrances to be overcome and eliminated before one gets into the fourth level of absorption (Jhana): this level is characterized by freedom from both physical sensations and mental feelings, by the absence of pleasurable sensation as well as distressing ones (*asukhamadukkham*), unruffled equanimity.

The level is described as 'absolute purity' resulting from mindful indifference (*upekkha-sati-parisuddhi*). The subject has neither the thrill of body and mind (*piti*), nor the joyous feeling (*sukha*). Both are looked upon as disturbances. A thirsty traveller is thrilled when he sights a lake and is joyous when he drinks water from it. But the experience of satisfaction that occurs thereafter is quiet and undistinguished. Consciousness at this level has the "steadiness of flame of lamp in the absence of wind".

THE SACRED VASE (KALASA), representing fulness of Wisdom. Used also in Tibet as one of the eight glorious emplems, *Bum-Pa.*

THE HUM MANDALA, used as a charm and employed in initiation rites.

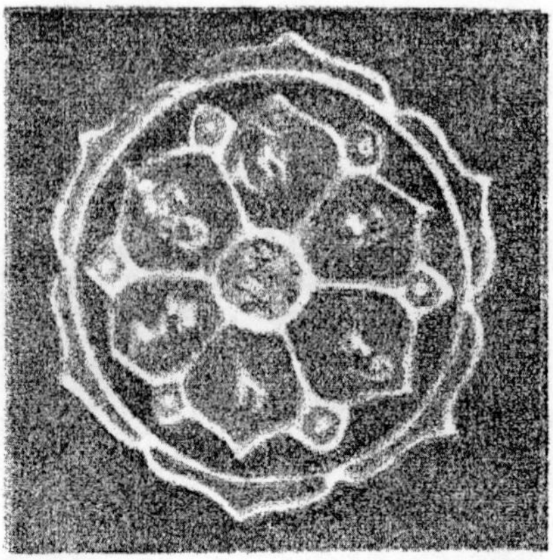

THE MANI-CHAKRA (with the formula *OM MANI PADME HUM HRIH* in Tibetan) used as a charm.

The practice that leads to this level of consciousness is technically known as samathabhavana (tranquillity meditation). It is a systematic cultivation or development of consciousness through its several levels so that there is an increasing clarity and intensity of consciousness; the purpose is to "present a picture of actually that is urged of any falsifications" (*nyanaponika thera*). This "bare awareness" is said to result in "clear comprehension", which is a tool for the final liberation that Buddhism envisages as a being for itself in this region of inwardness. This clear comprehension is followed by an insight into existence (vipassana). The Yoga also recognizes that "from mastery of mind-poise comes institution" (Patanjali, 3, 5). This is essentially a Tantric orientation.

MANTRA

In the practical disciplines of Tantrik persuasion the mantras (spells, charms, sacred words) occupy an important position. The expression 'mantra' is derived from two Sanskrit roots signifying 'to reflect' (man) and 'to protect' (rati). The import is that the mantra is a sacred word or formula that is capable of protecting the person that thinks of it or utters it. The very process of thinking or uttering is said to generate a saving power: it protects the person from existent or possible errors, calamities and misadventures. A whole science has developed in India concerning the source, course, employment and utility of the mantras, which number about seven crores. Known as Mantra-sastra, this subject is elaborately dealt with in several Kalpas, Patalas, Tantras and manuals (like Mantramahodadhi).

One of the celebrated Tantrik texts, Saradatilaka, contains an account of the origin of the mantra. It is based on the Kundalini theory. The store-house of psychic energy in the individual is of the nature of absolute sound (sabda-brahman). All the fifty letters of the Sanskrit alphabet, a to ksha, representing the fundamental propensities of man, are contained within it, indistinct and unperceived, as objects in darkness. Whenever there is an implusion to articulate a sound, a glimmer of light shines forth. The awareness of this impulsion and illumination is styled as 'spot' (bindu). Proceeding from the Kundalini in the Muladhara centre, it seeks to enter the arteries in order to obtain articulation. Before the entrance is gained, the sound is known as 'transcendent' (para). Its aspects are indistinguishable, and beyond ordinary apprehension.

Once it enters the arteries and begins to resound through them as far as the Svadhishthana centre, it is known as 'perceiving' (*pasyanti*). The mystic adepts can perceive it, although it is as yet beyond hearing. It is the 'visible sound'. When it reaches the throat (or in another account the heart, the anahata centre) it is called 'middling' or intermediate (*madhyama*): it is here both light and sound; the audible aspect more prominent. When it issues out of the throat and gets formed in the mouth it is pronounced or 'articulated' (*vaikhari*). All vocalized sound belongs to this last category: common speech as well as the mantras.

All speech has its foundation in the Om sound. As long as life lasts in the body, as long as the vital currents flow through the arteries, this primal sound is generated continuously. Any attempt to produce any sound instantaneously evokes the Om sound at the Anahata centre. Common speech, however, forces itself out of this source and operates purely at the intellectual level. The mantra, on the other hand, rests in the Om sound and works from that level.

The light aspect of the initial sound in the Muladhara centre is the seed from which the perceptible form of the deity (*devata*) emerges. Mantra is actually a technique by which the image of the deity is sought to be visualized. It is therefore that the deity is described as the visible mantra, and the mantra as the verbal deity. Each letter of the alphabet (*varna*) has a potency to evoke an aspect of the deity; and the mantra, composed of such letters (or syllables), would organize the individual potencies into

Some letters (syllables or phonemes) are capable of evoking the entire deity, and they are called 'seed-syllables' (*bija-aksharas*). The mantra is in fact an elaboration of a seed-syllable. The purpose of such elaboration is to assist in the visualization of the deity. It is said that the mantra without its seed-syllable will be incapable of benefitting even when repeated a lakh of times. Such a mantra is condemned as 'devoid of life-force'.

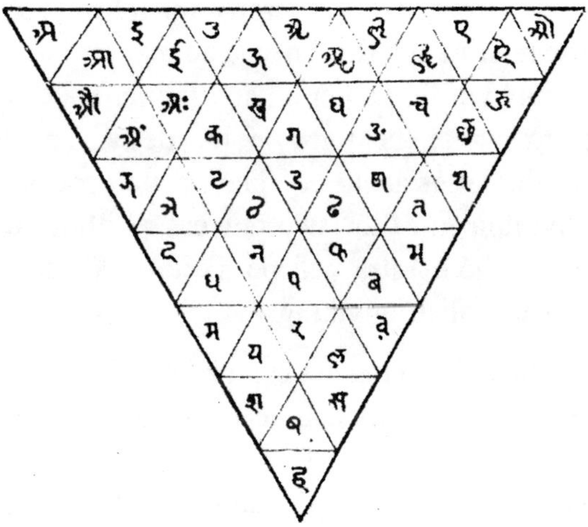

MANTRODDARA-YANTRA for constructing the appropriate mantra

The repetition of a mantra a hundred and eight times, or several thousand times, is meant to perfect the faculty of concentration whereby the elementary sound and the primal light fuse, making for reintegration of the psychophysical system. The repetition of a mantra is known as 'japa' (the Sanskrit word signifying both 'muttering' and 'thinking'). Three varieties of japa are recognized: (1) 'uttered' (*vacika*), audible to others; (2) 'muttered' (*upamsu*), audible to oneself only; and (3) 'thought of' (manasa), in entire silence, visualizing the deity of the mantra. We have it on the authority of Manu that the 'uttered' japa is ten times more efficacious than the rituals, the 'muttered' a hundred times better than" the 'uttered', and the 'thought of' a thousand times superior to the 'muttered'.

A special process of repetition of a mantra, known as 'purascarana' is resorted to at the commencement (purah, prior to) of any ritual or practice. The purpose is to bring before us (in front of us, purah) the close relationship between the mantra and the deity. The mantra has two kinds of powers: its own fundamental and inalienable power, and the power to evoke the form of the deity. The former is natural and the latter acquired. The above process is meant to secure the unison of the two powers. Without this initial establishment, the mantra will be like a sick person who is unable to accomplish anything.

It is insisted that a mantra can profit only when imparted ceremonially by a competent teacher (guru). Competence here means the achieved perfection in the employment of a mantra (*mantra-siddhi*), *viz.* the ability to readily evoke and freely utilize the deity from the mantra. The ritual of initiation into a mantra involves invoking the deity by the teacher in a ceremonial pot filled with consecrated water and five kinds of precious stones, performance of sacrifice in front of the pot, repetition of the mantra by the teacher 800 times with his right hand covering the mouth of the pot, bathing of the devotee with the water from the pot, and finally whispering of the mantra in the devotee's ear by the teacher.

The triad (the teacher, the mantra and the deity) are said to be indispensable in spiritual practice. The teacher symbolizes the devotee's soul, the mantra his mind, and the deity his vital current. It is only when the three come together that success is secured. It would be disadvantageous to look upon the teacher as a mere human being, the mantra as only an arrangement of syllables, or the deity as just an image in metal or stone. It is the attitude that determines the success of an enterprise. "All success is rooted in tradition and faith."

The mantras are thus spells or charms designed to bring about a desired benefit (*viniyoga*). They are devices to gather together the basic psychophysical forces both within the individual and outside him. The external form of the mantra consists of letters and words; sometimes nonsense-syllables may also enter; occasionally, meaningless words are introduced (as for instance, "cili cili" , "kulu kulu" "ade adau"). Some mantras contain syllables which are apparently impossible to pronounce: instances are hrsvphrom in the mantra for Hanuman, and Kshrvblum in the mantra for Matangi. Morc usually, however, the name or description of the deity is introduced in the dative case, along with an expression indication supplication (*namah*) or surrender (*svaha*).

Mantras are grouped into three varieties: 'male' when they end with words such as hum, phat, vashat; 'female', when they end with vaushat and svaha: and 'neuter', when they end with namah. The 'male' mantras are especially employed in magical rites, in the worship of ferocious divinities including goddesses, and in sorcery. They are said to be vigorous and quick in effect; but their spiritual value is minimal. The 'female' variety finds use in enterprises with concrete benefits as objectives. The 'neuter' mantras have spiritual progress as their goal. Mantras are also classified on the basis of the number of syllables they contain. If there is but a single syllable, it is called 'pinda-Mantra'; if two 'kartari'; if the number ranges from three to nine 'bija'; and where the number exceeds nine but is not more than twenty 'mantra'. If the number of syllables is more than twenty, the mantra becomes a 'mala-mantra' (*string-mantra*).

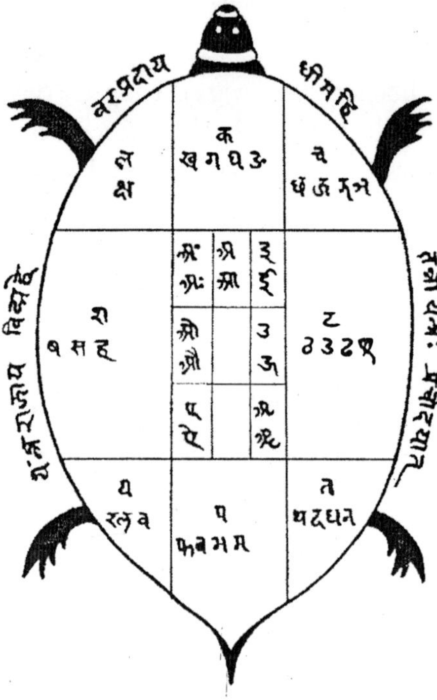

KURMA-CHAKRA for extracting mantras

For achieving perfection in the mantra, it is recommended that the mantra must be repeated as many lakhs of times as there are syllables in the mantra. And each day one is advised to stick to a specific but even number, and never for any reason exceed it or fall short of it.

The employment of a rosary is recommended to keep the count of repetitions. An elaborate system concerning the nature, material, consecration and use of the rosaries (japa-mala) has developed as an accessory to Mantra-sastra. The material from which the rosary is made depends upon the purpose of the mantra. If the purpose is general good and spiritual welfare, lotus-seeds, rudraksha berries or tulasi beads are employed. For success in an enterprise the rosary made of seeds of kusa-grass, coral or sandal wood is used. If the goal is great learning, crystal and pearls are used in the rosary; if perfection of dharma, conch-shell or precious stones; if attraction of affection, elephant tusks and bones; and in magical rites and sorcery the rosary is made from human skull, human bones or wood from a tree growing in a cemetery.

The rosary must be properly consecrated before it can be used effectively. And every time the rosary is used, it must priority be worshipped with its own mantra: aim drim akshamali-kayai namah. The rosary must have 108 beads, and while telling them in the morning the rosary must be placed near the navel, at noon near the heart and in the evening near the nose. The telling must be done by the right hand, and only the middle portion of the middle finger (or fore-finger) and the top portion of the thumb must hold the rosary; other parts of the hand must not come into contact with the rosary while it is in use. And while telling the bead, the hands as well as the rosary should be concealed in a loose pouch known as 'go-mukhi', or by cloth. When not in use, the rosary should be secreted in a place of worship; it should never be worn on the body or shown to people.

Often times, a mantra which is to be accomplished is inscribed on bhurja-leaf or on a metal (gold, silver, or copper) sheet: alternately, it is written on a paper with materials such as sandal paste, incense or turmeric powder and milk.

In magic and sorcery, blood is used for writing. It is usual to enclose the mantra in an appropriate diagram (*yantra*), e.g. a lotus with eight or six or a hundred petals (each petal containing a syllable of the mantra) a triangle, circle, or square with doorways on its sides. This diagram is duly worshipped before the japa commences.

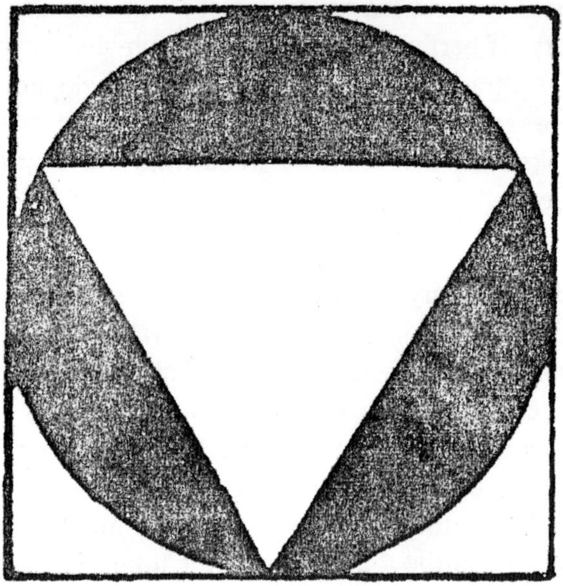

Simple YANTRA for installing the ritual vase (Kalasa) before worship

The total number of possible mantras is placed at seven crores. Some texts give the number more precisely as 67, 108, 863. Of course, a large majority of them are either impossible to use, or are defective for one reason or another. There are about 3,000 mantras that have been talked about in texts. They are grouped in two major classes: benign (*dakshina*) and malevolent (*vama*). The former, more commonly used, involve benevolent and peaceful divinities and rituals of a pacific type; they preclude all injury, violence and ill-will. The usual benefits sought are prosperity, long life, health, worldly success, and spiritual progress.

The malevolent mantras, on the other hand, are employed in black magic, sorcery and witchcraft. The activities under this head are six-fold: pacification of spirits which otherwise would be harmful (*santi*), securing the affection of one desired (*vasikarana*) restraining one from an intended act (*stambhana*), removal of an enemy from his vantage position (*uccatana*), creating enmity between two powerful friends (*vidveshana*), and destruction of an enemy (*marane*). Many are the treatises that deal elaborately with the mantras that are used in this context, the methods of employment and the gruesome rites that must accompany them. This is the dark aspect of the Mantra-sastra which gave it the bad name.

A few specimens of the commonly used mantras are given in the following pages. The credulous and over-enthusiastic reader needs to be cautioned that no mantra is said to become useful unless properly communicated by a competent teacher, and unless repeated several thousand times over, with single-minded devotion. A mantra taken from a book will not only be utterly useless but positively disturb!

SPECIMENS OF MANTRAS

1. Mantra of Hanuman for safety and elimination of evil forces. *Om namo bhagavate Anjaneyaya mahabalaya svaha; Om aim srim hram hrim hrum hrsphom hrsphem hrsphaum hum phat.*

   or *Ham Hanumate namah.*

2. Mantra of Krishna for success and prosperity:

   Klim Krishnaya namah.

3. Mantra of Durga for victory over inimical forces: *Om hrim dum Durgayai namah.*

4. Mantra of Sudarsana (the discus-deity attending on Vishnu) for destroying undesirable influences and for procuring all-round protection:

   Om Sahasrara hum phat.

   or *Sudarsanaya vidmahe, mahajvalaya dhimahi, tan nas cakrah procadayat (gayatri).*

5. Mantra of Kali for safety and success (in gayatri metre):

   Om hrim Adyayai vidmahe, paramesvaryai dhimahi tan no Kali pracodayat.

6. Mantra of Vishnu for healing a sick person:

   Om hrim hram rim ram Vishnusaktaye namah; Om namo Vishnusakti om hara hara naya naya paca paca matha matha, utsadaya dure kuru svaha: himavantam gaccha jiva sah sah sah candra-mandalagato' si svaha.

7. Mantra for attracting nectar (long life)

   Om amrite amritavarshini amritam sravaya sravaya sam sam klim klim hrum hrum hram hram hrim hrim dravaya dravaya svaha.

8. Mantra for perfection in learning:

   Om cala cala cili cili culu culu kulu kulu mulu mulu hum hum hum hum phat phat phat phat Padmahaste svaha.

9. Mantra of Ganapati to overcome death and disaster:

   Om namo Ganapataye mahavira mrityum hana hana dhama dhama matha matha; kalam samhara samhara; sarvagrahams cumaya cumaya; nagan motaya motaya: Rudrarupa sarvato-mukha hum phat svaha.

10. Mantra of Krishna (Santanagopala) for progeny:

    Om namo bhagavate jagatprasutaye namah.

11. Mantra of Narasimha for protection from disaster:

    Om hrim kshraum krom hum phat.

12. Mantra of Garuda for cure of snake-bite:

    Kshipa om svaha.

13. Mantra of Vatuka-bhairava for strength in the midst of trouble:

Om srim hrim klim kshrmyum Vatukaya apaduddharanaya kuru kuru Vatukaya hrim.

14. Mantra of Dakshinamurti for wisdom:

    Om a namas Sivaya a Om.

15. Mantra of Hayagriva for eloquence.

    Hsum Hayasirase namah.

16. Mantra of Varahi for preventing bad dreams:

    Aim hrim nama varahi aghore svapne tha tha tha tha svaha.

17. Mantra of Camundi for extinction of enemies:

    Om hrim phat Rakta-camundesvari satrujivitanasini ehyehi sighram ishtanakarshayakarshaya svaha.

18. Mantra of Lakshmi for prosperity:

    Om srim klim Mahalakshmi ehyehi sarvasaubhagyam me dehi svaha.

19. Mantra of Dhanvantari as antidote to all ailments:

    Om nama bhagavate Dhanvantaraye amritakala sahastaya sarvamaya vinasaya Vishnave svaha.

20. Mantra for securing clairaudition :

    Om hrim Karna-pisaci me kame kathaya hrum phat svaha.

REFERENCES

1. *Rgveda* 10.71.9 "Ta ete vacamabhipadya papaya tiris tantram tanvate," Sayana explains: "tantram krshilakshanam tanvate, vistarayanti, kurvanti".
2. *Atharva-veda* 10.7.42 "tantram eke yuvati, etc".
3. *Ashtadhayi*, 5.2.70.
4. *Apastamba Srauta-sutra*, 1, 51, 1, where 'tantra' is defined by the commentator as 'angasamudayah'.
5. Sabara on Jaimini's *Purva-Mimamsa-sutra* 11.4.1: "Yat sakritkrtam bahunam upakaroti, yatha brahmananam madhye krtah pradipah." Also Sankhayana-Srauta-sutra 1.16.6 commentary: 'Vat sakrt krtam bahunam upakaroti tat tantram ity ucyate.'
6. Isvarakrshna's *Samkhyakarika,* 70 'tena ca bahudha krtam tantram'; Samkara on Brahma-sutra, 2, 2, 1.
7. *Bhagavata*, 1, 3, 8.
8. *Arthasastra,* Adhikarana 15 (Tantrayukti), cf; also Caraka (12, 36 'tantrasya yuktayah') and Susruta (Uttara-tantra, 65, 32).
9. *Kulluka-bhatta* (between 1150 and 1300) on Manu 2, 1. 'Srutis ca dvividha, vaidiki tantriki ca',
10. *e.g. Agni Purana*, 372, 34 and *Bhagavata,* 11th Skandha: 'Vaidiki tantriki misra iti trividho makhah'.
11. *e.g. Kakacandesvara-mata* : 'vedanam ca vayorthena na siddhistena jayate' (The Vedas being old cannot lead to attainment).
12. Commentary on *Yajnavalkya-samhita*, p. 19.
13. *e.g.* in Bhaskara-raya's *Setubandha*, p. 5, cf *Sukarnitisara*, 4, 3, 39: 'atharvanam c'opavedas tantranpah sa evahi:
14. *Mundukopanishad*, 1, 4.
15. *Brahma-sutra-bhashya* 1, 4, 14; also 'vedantartha-sampradaya-vit', Ibid. 2, 1, 9. Two others, *viz.,* Sundarapandya and Dravida-

carya, are also described as 'knowers of Tradition' (*Gita- bhashya,* 3.12 and *Brhadaranyaka-bhashya,* 2.1.20). But their works have not survived.

16. *Bhagavad-Gita-bhashya,* 3, 2.
17. cf. R. Sama Sastri, *Ind. Anti.,* 1906, pp. 262.
18. *Chandogya-bhashya,* 2.23.1.
19. Haraprasad Sastri, Lama Anagarika Govinda and David Snellgrove thought 'Sandhabhasha' was corrupt for 'sandhya-bhasha' (twilight language). But Vidhusekhara Bhattacharya and Prabodhachandra Bagchi hold that 'sandha' is correct form from the gerund of 'dha', prefixed by 'sam' (*sandhaya bhasha,* in the sense of *abhipretya, uddisya,* 'aiming at', 'denoting', 'intending'.
20. *cf. Kularnava-tantra:* 'Mano'nyatra Sivo'nyatra saktir anyatra maratuh; na siddhyati Vararohe Kalpakoti satair api'.
21. cf. Guiseppe Tucci, *Theory and Practice of the Mandala* (London, Rider, 1960), Ajit Mukerjee, Tantra Art (1968), C.A. Muses *The Esoteric Teachings of Tibetan Tantra* (Colorado, Indiana Hills, 1961), Herbert Guenther, Treasures on the Tibetan Middle Way (Berkeley, 1969), Ralph Metzer. *Maps of Consciousness* (New York, 1971).
22. *Yogavasishtha* : 'Jivasya trini rupani sthula-sukshma-parani ca, sthulam pani-padamayam bhogartham, sukshman svasam-kalpa-mayakaram, param adyantarahitam sat yam cin-matram nirvikal-pakam'.
23. They are located at the big toe (*padangushtha*), heel (*parshni*), ankle (*gulpha*), knee (*janu*), anus (*guda*), 'sacral plexus' (*mula-dhara*), perineum (*yonisthana*), testes (*mushka*), genital organ (*medhra*), groin (*vamksama*), 'prostate plexus' (*svadhishthana*), bulb-nest (*kundayoni*), navel (*nabhi*), 'solar plexus' (*manipura*), thumb (*angushtha*), elbow (*aratni*), arm-pit (*kaksha*), heart (*anahata*), tip of the tongue (*jihvagra*), back of the throat (*visuddha*), soft palate (ghantika), uvular palate (*talu*), tip of the nose (*nasagra*), middle of the eye-brows (*bhru-madhya*), just above this area (*ajna*), in between the above two (*lalana*), near the ajna (mind, *manas*) about the mideranial region (*soma*), and on top the cranium (*sahasrara*).
24. The Centers are pictured as lotuses each with a specific number of petals, and on the petals are mentioned various seed-syllables. From muladhara to ajna, the number of petals are in order 4, 6,

10, 12, 16 and 2 (altogether 50 corresponding to the letters of the alphabet). For details of this psycholinguistic mysticism see *Rudrayamala,* patala 17, verses 50 ff. and Purnananda's *Shatcakranirupana.*

25. cf. John Woodroffe : *The Serpent Power* (Madras, 1953) and other works, V.G. Rele, *The Mysterious Kundalini* (Bombay, 1927), M.P. Pandit *Kundalini Yoga* (Madras, 1959), M.R. Datta, *The Secret Serpent Power* (Dacca, 1913), C. Chakrabarty, Cultural *History of Hindus* (Calcutta, 1945), Agehananda Bharati, *The Tantrik Tradition* (1970), Philip Rawson, *The Art of the Tantra.*

26. Bhaskara-raya's *Saubhagyabhaskara,* Comm. on Lalita-*sahasranama,* verses 87-91. "sa hi muladharakhya-cakre sardhatrivalayakarena supta sati yogibhir utthapya shatcak-rani Brahma-vishnvadigranthims ca bhedayanti Sahasraram nita sati tatkarnikarupacandra-mandalad amrtam sravayati." Saradatilaka 25, 65 contains a beautiful description of Kundalini's passage to *Sahasrara* and return to *Muladhara.*

27. *Devibhagavata,* 11, 1, 47 "Prakasamanam prathame prayane pratiprayanepyamrtayamanam".

28. *Yogacudamani-Upanishad:* "Shatsatani divaratrau sahasrany-ekavimsatih; etat samkhyanvitam mantram jivo japati sarvada"; cf. also "Hakarena bahiryati sakarena viset punah; hamsatmikam bhagavatim jivo japati sarvada" ; *Hamsopanisad,* "So' ham hamsapadenaiva jivo japati sarvada". The japa here is described as 'ajapajapa'.

29. *Kularnava-tantra,* 14, 93 "vina diksham na mokshah syat taduktam sivasasane; sa ca syad vinacaryyam ity acaryyapa-rampara".

30. *Ibid.* 14, 97.

31. "Divyabhavapradanac ca kshalanat kalmasasya ca: diksheti kathita sadbhir bhavabandha-vimocanat" (*Kularnava*); cf. also *Prapancasara,* 5, 2.

32. *Parasurama-kalpasutra,* 1, 12 "prakatyan nirayah". cf. also *Saktisangama-tantra,* 36, 24 f "Suguptam Kaulikacaram anugrhnanti devatah; vanchasiddhim prayacchanti nasayanti prakasane".

33. "Na nama-jati-vicaro' sti no'cchishtadivivecanam; cakrad vinihsrtah salve svavarnasramo'ditan; lokayatraprasidd-hyartham kuryuh karma prthak prthak" (*Mahaniivana-tantra,* 8, 180-197).

34. *Lakshmidhara* on *Saundaryalahari,* verse 10 "Samayacaro nama antarapujaratih, kulacaro nama bahyapujaratir iti rahasyam.....

Samayinam mantrasya purascaranam nasti, japo nasti, bahyahomo'pi nasti, bahyapujavidhayo na santyeva. Hrtkamala eva sarvam yavad anushtheyam".

35. *Ibid.* "Gurumukhavedyah samayacarah".
36. Vamakesvara-tantra, 51 "antaryagatmijka puja sarvapujottama priye; bahih puja vidhatavya yavaj jnanam na jayate".
37. *Ibid.* "bhavo hi manaso dharmo mansaiva sadabhayaset" cf "Sakti-pradnanyat beavanam trayanom sadhakasya ca; divyavira-pasunam ca bhavatrayam udahrtam".
38. "Sariram trividham proktam attamadhama-mandhyemam". cf. also "Paranande mate trayo margah-dakshinah, vamah, uttaran na dakshinad uttamam vamam, vamad uttaram uttamam, uttaran na kvacit".
39. The seven-fold conduct is necessitated because human nature is not uniform; Vedacara (Vedic rituals), Vaishnavacara (Pauranik rituals), dakshinacara (the worship of the Goddess by employing Vedic hymns), vamacara (secret worship of the goddess with the five 'm's : madya, mamsa, mudra, matsya and maithuna), saivacara (Saivite rituals following Vedic tradition), siddhantacara (ecstatic rites in the burning grounds) and kaulacara (unfettered and wisdom-dominated rituals). The last, which is considered the best, is identified with Yoga ("Yogamargam Kaulamargam ekacara kramam prabho! Yogi bhutva kulam dhyatva sarvasiddhesvaro bhavet").
40. Saivagama : "panthano bahavah proktah mantra-sastra-manishibhih; svaguror matam asritya subham karyam na canyatha".
41. "Sarve ca pasavas santi talavad bhutale nrnam".
42. What follows is an account from Sarada-tilaka, 1, 7, 8.
43. Sivapurana (Vayaviya-samhita) "Sivecchaya para-saktih Sivatattvaikatam gata; tatah prasphuratyadau tailam tilad iva".
44. cf. Tantraloka. 3,136-148.
45. ct. S.N. Dasgupta "A General Introduction to Tantras", Asutosh Mookerji Silver Jubilee Volume III, pt. I, 1922.
46. cf. Sarvajnanottara-tantra, gloss: "Kundalini sabdavacyastu bhujangakutilakarena nadatmana svakaryena pratipurusam bhedenavasthito na tu svarupena pratipurusham avasthitah".
47. For details, see Gopinath Kaviraj : Aspects of Indian Thought, University of Burdwan, 1966, Chapter on "Sakta Philosophy".

48. *Siddahasiddhantasangraha,* 3, 40 "akhandaparipurnatma visvarupo mahesvarah; ghate ghate citprakasas tisthati.... "

49. *Siddhasiddhanta-paddhati* "Saiva saktih yada sahajena svatunmilinya nirutthanadasayam vartate tada sivah sa eva bhavati".

50. *Saktisangama-tantra, Kalikhanda,* 3, 22: "Sri-Kalyapesaka ye ca tat kulam parikirtitam". Kula is variously interpreted as Sakti (Kulam Saktir iti proktam), one's own body (Kulam sari ram mahaprayojanahetutaya jneyam, yesham te kulah" *Yoginihrdaya-dipika* 2, 78), and family lineage (sva-sva-vamsa paramparaprapto margah").

51. *Ibid*, Tarakhanda, 36, 25. "Suguptam kaulikacaram anugrh-nanti devatah".

52. Ramesvara's comm. on *Parasurama-kalpasutra* h.153.

53. The *purvakaulas* draw a triangle and worship the point in its center, or they worship the Sricakra; the uttarakaulas on the other hand, worship the actual vulva of a young maid; others both. Lakshmidhara in his comm. on Saundaryalahari, verse 41, adds "Much can be written on this; but because they are so outlandish they are not fit even to be remembered".

54. "antah Saktah bahih Saivah sabhayam Vaishnava matah, nanavesadhara kaulah vicaranti mahitale", *Kaulavalinirnaya,* 10, 85.

55. Samyutta-Nikaya, Sagathavagga, 4, 19.

56. *Ibid.*, Khandavagga, 1, 53.

57. *Mundaka-Upanishad*, 2, 2, 8.

58. *Katha-Upanishad,* 1, 2, 1.

59. *Ibid.*, 2, 2, 12.

60. *Visuddhimagga,* 8, 189-226.